Staff Development

A PRACTICAL GUIDE

second edition

Prepared by the
Staff Development Committee
Personnel Administration Section
Library Administration and Management Association
American Library Association

Coordinating Editors
Anne Grodzins Lipow
and
Deborah A. Carver

American Library Association
Chicago and London 1992

Cover designed and composed by Donavan Vicha on Atari TT030-based *PageStream* publishing system and output on Varityper VT600 laser printer. Interior text designed and composed by Donavan Vicha on 386 DR DOS-based *Ventura Publisher* 3.0 in Garamond and Optima and output on a Varityper VT600 laser printer.

Printed on 50-pound Finch Opaque, a pH-neutral stock, and bound in 10-pt C1S cover stock by McNaughton & Gunn Lithographers.

The paper used in this publication meets the minimum requirements of American National Standard for Information Sciences—Permanence of Paper for Printed Library Materials, ANSI Z39.48-1984. ∞

Library of Congress Cataloging-in-Publication Data

Staff development : a practical guide / prepared by the Staff Development Committee, Personnel Administration Section, Library Adminstration and Management Association, American Library Association ; coordinating editors, Anne Grodzins Lipow and Deborah A. Carver. — 2nd ed.
      p.   cm.
   Includes bibliographical references and index.
   ISBN 0-8389-3402-1
   1. Library education (Continuing education) 2. Library employees—Training of. 3. Library personnel management. I. Lipow, Anne. II. Carver, Deborah A. III. Library Administration and Management Association. Staff Development Committee.
   Z668.5.S 1991
   020'.71'5—dc20   91-18962
                                                                     CIP

Printed in the United States of America

95 94 93 92   5 4 3 2

Contents

PART I. CONCEPTS

PART II. METHODS

PLANNING

Introduction

Staff development may be one of the most important and widely recognized needs in libraries. A few large university and public libraries have staff-development officers who devote their time and expertise to planning programs and workshops that are relevant to the needs and interests of the library staff. In the vast majority of libraries, however, staff development is a responsibility which is shared among many librarians and supervisors who have a wide range of other duties and assignments. Many of us have found ourselves in a position where we want or need to develop a program, but we are not sure how to proceed through all the stages of planning, preparing, and implementation.

In response to the growing interest and concern among many librarians who wanted more practical advice, the Staff Development Committee of the Personnel Administration Section (PAS), Library Administration and Management Association (LAMA), presented a program entitled "Staff Development: Practical Approaches to Getting Started" at the 1986 Annual Conference of the American Library Association (ALA). A brochure listing tips for starting a program was distributed to the audience. As they indicated in their evaluations, the participants found this brochure to be extremely useful. The committee decided to prepare a series of similar brochures, which evolved into the first edition of this publication in 1988.

The first edition sold out quickly and remains one of the best-selling LAMA publications. The reader-response forms that were returned to the committee were all positive. Many of our readers suggested that we include descriptions of some of the fundamental staff-development concepts. In this new edition, chapters 1 through 5 provide a background on a few basic principles such as adult-learning theory, transfer of training, and instructional design. In addition to this new section, more information has been added to the Methods section, including chapters on improving visual aids, making effective presentations, and developing training skills.

In producing this guide, the committee is executing its charge "to facilitate and promote effective staff development programs in order to maximize staff abilities to perform successfully their responsibilities and thereby improve overall library effectiveness." Perhaps our primary audience will consist of library personnel who are still relatively new to staff development, but we hope that those with plenty of experience will find some useful advice as well. Even libraries with staff-development officers might use the text to help smaller units within the organization gain an understanding of the "hows, whats, and wheres" of staff development.

For permission to reprint their staff-development policy statements, we thank the University of California, Berkeley; Palatine Public Library District, Illinois; Regent University, Virginia; the University of Texas, Austin; Riverside City and County Public Library, California; Indiana University, Bloomington; the Massachusetts Institute of Technology; and the University of Michigan. For permission to include their staff-development surveys, we thank the Tacoma Public Library and the University of Michigan.

It is a pleasure to acknowledge the efforts of past and present Staff Development Committee chairs who helped to encourage and organize this publication: Charles E. Kratz, J. Linda Williams, and Melissa Carr. Special thanks to Marilyn Murray and Angela Vogel of the Baltimore County Public Library and to Julie Janisse of the University of Oregon, who spent many painstaking hours keying, reformatting, and proofing text from a wide array of disks and word-processing programs.

Deborah A. Carver
Anne Grodzins Lipow
Coordinating Editors

How to Use This Book

The first five chapters of this book are intended to give the reader a theoretical background to many of the chapters which appear in the second section. The second section (chapters 6 through 19) is designed to be read piecemeal, depending upon where you and your library are in your staff-development efforts: planning, preparing a new program design, or continuing and expanding on existing programs. If, however, you begin at the beginning and read through to the end, you will gain an important conceptual overview. You will also notice some repetition of ideas—although, in each instance, the idea is presented from a different perspective or within a different context. This repetition is intentional. Because the stages of staff development do not separate neatly into discrete, unconnected segments, the authors were free to discuss their topics without regard to overlap. The result is that the reader can get, from a single chapter, an independent but rounded discussion of an aspect of staff development.

Also, the design of the page allows you, the reader, to add your own annotations, thus making you, in a sense, a coauthor. If this is your personal copy, use the wide space to the left of the text to record your observations and experiences, references to your personal documents, or whatever else would transform the book's messages into your own thoughts and words.

Finally, if this book turns out to be helpful to you in a particular way, or if you have suggestions for improvements, and especially if you catch an error, the LAMA PAS Staff Development Committee would appreciate hearing from you. Please send your comments to:

Staff Development: A Practical Guide
c/o LAMA Executive Director
American Library Association
50 East Huron Street
Chicago, IL 60611

PART I   CONCEPTS

1   How People Learn: Applying the Adult Learning Model to Training Sessions

Susan Jurow

Andragogy is the term coined to describe the study of adult learning. Over the past half century, a body of literature has emerged detailing the research in this field. Trainers of adult learners need to have a basic understanding of what has been discovered about how adults learn and of what these findings imply for the way training programs should be designed and conducted.

The central issue requires us to shift our thinking from an emphasis on "teaching" to "learning." The bulk of our learning experiences have been as children or young adults, where our job was to absorb knowledge from the teacher. As a result, we tend to see the person at the front of the room as the key player in our learning experience. For adult learners, the issue becomes how to integrate what is heard and seen with the lifetime of experience and knowledge already in place. The trainer's ability to facilitate this process is the key to a successful learning experience for the adult.

Characteristics of the Adult Learner

Malcolm Knowles, professor emeritus at North Carolina State University, Raleigh, has studied and written extensively in the area of adult education and human-resource development. He is a leader in the development of adult-learning theory. There are five assumptions he considers key to understanding the adult-learning process.

1. Adults are accustomed to being in control and taking responsibility for their own lives. Most people like to think of themselves as independent and self-directed. They often feel uncomfortable when

1

placed in situations where they have little control or feel challenged by their lack of knowledge.

2. Adults bring personal experience to the learning activity. Experience is the core of the adult's sense of self. It can be converted into new knowledge and understanding with appropriate learning structures, and it can serve as a rich resource for the learner to share with others.

3. Adults are ready to learn when they need to know something. The desire to seek a learning situation springs most often from a need to be more effective. It may be sparked by a problem that needs to be solved, or it may be triggered by a change that has occurred in the individual's personal life or career.

4. Adults want to use their knowledge to accomplish something. Adults expect what they learn to be relevant to their needs. They expect to see the connection between the material being presented and the problem they are trying to solve or the task they have undertaken.

5. Adults seek learning experiences that will help them meet internal needs. Abraham Maslow and Frederick Herzberg referred to the need for self-esteem, recognition, and self-actualization as internal or higher level needs. Once our most basic needs for food and shelter are satisfied, these higher level goals are likely to be more powerful motivators than what Maslow and Herzberg called external needs, such as better pay or job security.

Creating a Climate for Learning

The concerns that Knowles outlines have implications for the kinds of programs that are likely to be effective for the adult learner. It is of primary importance that the trainer create an environment conducive to learning. Several conditions that relate to the relationship between the learner and the trainer, as well as to the relationship among the learners themselves, can facilitate the learning process. These conditions include the level of participation, respect, collaboration, reflection and practice, and empowerment.

Participation

Participation in a learning event should be voluntary. If participation is demanded, the individual may sense a loss of control, which can result in feelings of resentment and resistance to the learning process. Also, if the individual does not feel the need to learn the particular concepts covered in the training program, it is unlikely that much will be retained.

The trainer should look for ways to involve the learners as much as possible in the needs assessment and the formulation of training and staff-development objectives. Active participation can foster a sense of ownership in the planned program. This sense of ownership of the content of the learning event can increase the learner's commitment to its success.

Respect

A climate of mutual respect provides the groundwork for a situation where new ideas can be freely debated and discussed. Participation in discussion and learning activities increases when the value of each individual's experience is acknowledged and accepted.

Collaboration

For learners to be able to take advantage of the personal experience of others, the traditional spirit of competition must be replaced with a sense of shared responsibility for the quality of the common learning experience. The trainer can encourage collaboration by providing opportunities for participants to respond to the inquiries of others, to suggest resources which they have found useful, and to express personal points of view.

Reflection and Practice

For adults to acquire and fully integrate desired knowledge or skills, the learning process must involve personal discovery. New ideas should be presented in such a way that learners are free to explore the merits and defects and to compare them with their own view of how things work. This type of examination will often lead to new insights with new applications. If ideas are presented as universal truths, the adult may focus too much on searching his or her entire history for experiences or events which prove otherwise.

An effective training program provides opportunities for both discussion and practice. The adult learner may have to struggle with internal and external resistance to change. For most adult learners, it will be helpful if skills can be practiced in the open and accepting environment of the workshop.

Empowerment

The role of the trainer is to help the learner learn. The trainer should also encourage the learner to remain enthusiastic and interested in the learning process after the program is over. The same techniques that promote participation, respect, collaboration, and reflection and practice also support the ability of the adult to continue to take responsibility for learning following the program's conclusion.

Programs That Support Adult Learning

Most people learn as naturally as they breathe. Learning is the continuous, natural process by which people examine what happens to them and draw generalizations from that experience. These generalizations enable individuals to deal with similar situations more easily in the future.

A model that often is used to describe the four stages of the learning process of adults is shown in figure 1. In stage one, an event happens. In stage two, the individual considers what has occurred and reflects on any subsequent reaction. In stage three, the individual compares this event with previous situations and tries to understand what it means. In stage four, the individual responds to a new situation using knowledge or understanding gained from this recent experience. The process of experimentation leads to a new experience, and the cycle begins again.

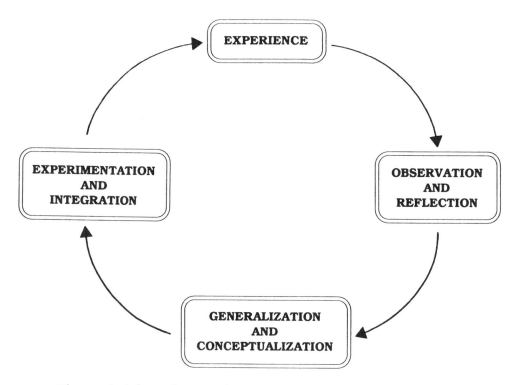

Figure 1. A learning model

We can incorporate these four stages into the structure of our staff-development and training programs. Rather than lecturing to a group of adults and having them begin the learning process by questioning your wisdom and authority, start the training session by engaging participants in an activity. Effective activities can include working through a case study, role playing, completing a self-analysis survey, or attempting to solve a problem. This activity corresponds to the initial event in the learning model.

After this activity has been completed, engage the learners in a discussion of what occurred and what their personal reactions were to this event. Help them to structure the information, so that they can see themes or patterns in their observations.

At this point the group is ready to look for connections or similarities between the dynamics of the activity and their day-to-day lives. The trainer can assist the adult learner in this process by presenting models and research findings that confirm or contradict the participants' shared experiences. In other words, the trainer is guiding the learning process.

The last step is the most important. While the experience and discussion are fresh in their minds, help the learners consider ways of applying their new knowledge to their own lives. They can practice their new skills in a role play that will help them adapt new behavior to the workplace.

You may want to provide them with a structure that will help them to set goals that reflect the changes or improvements they would like to make. The trainer can also give the learners an opportunity to share these goals with others and, perhaps, have them agree to help each other as they attempt to implement their ideas.

Conclusion

If we are to use the adult-learning model effectively as a basis for our training programs, the roles and responsibilities of the trainer and the learner need to be clear to each of them. The learner is responsible for identifying personal needs and for seeking appropriate training. The learner brings energy, enthusiasm, and a lifetime of experience to the learning process, which fuels the workshop. The trainer's role is to provide content that will meet the learner's needs and a structure that will enable the learner to acquire the desired knowledge.

2 How People Apply What They Learn: Transfer of Training

Deborah A. Carver

Transfer of training refers to the individual's ability to apply new procedures or behaviors learned in the classroom to the workplace. Successful transfer involves the acquisition, application, and retention of new skills. Most professionals in the field of human-resource development (HRD) would agree that training is worthwhile only if successful transfer occurs. In terms of cost-benefit ratios, it makes little sense to invest the time and expense of training and staff-development programs if no measurable improvements in job performance and satisfaction result. However, most HRD professionals would also agree that the incidence of successful transfer is alarmingly low. Recent estimates indicate that more than $100 billion dollars and 15 billion work hours are spent annually on training programs but that as little as 10 percent of the expenditures result in long-term behavior change (Wexley and Baldwin 1986, 503).

The recent interest in transfer-of-training issues may be a result of a precarious economy, slumping productivity, and rapid technological advances requiring new skills and expertise. As the nature of our work becomes more complex and demanding, the need for highly skilled employees becomes increasingly critical. Many libraries have responded to these needs by instituting a series of training and staff-development programs. Unfortunately, our efforts do not always produce the desired changes. At best, only 40 percent of any training program's content will transfer immediately. After one year, noticeable application of new skills is likely to drop by another 25 percent (Newstrom 1986, 34).

Barriers to Transfer of Training

Why do many training programs fail to produce the desired results? There are a number of plausible explanations for this phenomenon. We sometimes fail to see training programs as a means to an end. We make the mistake of assuming that if we are taught how to do something, we can and will do it. A training program is doomed if we fail to recognize its vulnerability. Therefore, the first and most important step toward improving transfer of training is to admit that it is not automatic.

There are both psychological and organizational barriers to transfer. Frequently, participants either lack confidence in their ability to successfully use the new skills on the job or feel that the values being taught are contrary to existing organizational values. Managers may take a passive attitude toward change and fail to reinforce and reward new behavior. They may not know enough about the skills being taught to identify appropriate changes in job performance. Managers may also fail to reach a mutual understanding with participants as to the desired outcomes (Trost 1985, 79).

Transfer can be defeated during the training session. Many programs fail to break down complex skills into component parts. For example, conflict management requires several basic skills, including the ability to listen, analyze, and handle stressful situations. If the program is too general, the participants will have difficulty knowing how and when to use specific behaviors. New skills can also fail to transfer if there is insufficient time allowed for classroom practice.

Training and staff-development programs often fail to produce results because there is no follow-up to ensure long-term maintenance of behavior. New skills require a trial-and-error process. Trainees who are unprepared to cope with mistakes may become discouraged and abandon the new approach when desired results are not immediately evident.

What approaches can be taken to overcome these barriers to transfer? Although most attention has focused on the design and content of the training sessions, successful transfer of skills requires that certain actions be taken before, during, and after the training program.

Ensuring Positive Transfer of Training

Program Preparation

Some studies have indicated that even when all the prerequisite motor and cognitive skills are present, performance will be poor if motivation is absent (Noe 1986, 737). Motivation is greater, and transfer of training more likely to occur, if the program is closely matched to the participants' needs. Too often, employees are asked to attend a generic training session that may have little relevance to their jobs. When employees are required to attend a workshop and the reasons are unclear, there may be a lack of motivation or even active resistance to learning.

Participants should be informed of the program's objectives. If they have realistic expectations and know why they have been selected to participate, the program will be more successful. Some advance work, such as introductory reading or self-assessment surveys, will help to prepare the trainees. A pretraining contract can be issued by the trainer specifying what new skills will be learned and what benefits will result if these skills are used on the job.

The work environment must also be examined to determine barriers that may impede transfer. For example, a library wants to do a program on effective reference-question negotiation. The required skills take time to acquire, but the trainer discovers that the reference desk is understaffed and that the librarians feel pressured to answer questions quickly. In this case, environmental conditions will make it difficult for participants to apply the skills taught in the training program. Although empirical evidence is scant, many HRD professionals believe that organizational climate is the most prevalent factor affecting transfer (Newstrom 1986, 37). If significant environmental barriers exist, that particular training program should probably be canceled.

The extent of management support has a major influence on the results of a training program. A lack of support is a common reason why skills learned in the classroom fail to transfer to the workplace. Without management's endorsement, training is more likely to be perceived as a break from work and little else. It is crucial that trainers understand the role that managers play in the transfer process and involve them in the planning and preparation stages.

Finally, the participants' initial perceptions of the trainer and the content of the course will affect the degree of transfer. If the trainer is not a credible expert, or if the content of the course is viewed with some skepticism, transfer of training will be minimal (Noe 1986, 742).

Program Implementation

Transfer will depend upon the structure and content of the training program. One common error is to include too much in the program rather than focusing on one or two select skills. A series of short programs ordered in logical progression is often more effective than a single marathon session. If more than one skill is being taught in a single session, negative transfer can occur if the second skill is introduced before the first is mastered (Kelley, Orgel, and Baer 1985, 79–80).

The training program should include theory as well as practical instruction. The principles must be illustrated with appropriate examples that are identical to those occurring in the job environment. If the examples are foreign to the participants, they may reject the principles, and future skill application is unlikely (Leifer and Newstrom 1980, 43). The training program must also give participants an opportunity to practice new skills in the classroom. Hands-on instruction helps participants understand when and how to use new skills.

It is less difficult to ensure the transfer of technical and motor skills than behavioral skills. With motor skills, applicable situations are easily identified, and the desired results are virtually guaranteed (Leifer and Newstrom 1980, 42). Most librarians know that it is easier to teach a new circulation clerk how to check out a book than to deal effectively with an angry patron. For this reason, trainers should put special emphasis on the applicability of behavioral and cognitive skills, such as the ability to detect, understand, and remedy a morale problem. If a new skill is applied at the wrong time, the lack of positive results may discourage further effort.

While procedural tasks may be easier to teach, they can still be forgotten after a period of time unless adequate practice occurs during the training session. In one study on procedural tasks described by Joel D. Schendel and Joseph D. Hagman (1982), participants were divided into three groups. One group received overtraining, i.e., repeated practice beyond the first successful performance of a skill. Participants in this group performed better several weeks after the training session than participants who did not practice or practiced only briefly. This and other studies on the effects of overtraining suggest that it is a worthwhile approach to enhance the transfer process.

Trainers should also encourage participants to discuss their experience and observations following practice sessions. Some theorists have argued that the advent of instructional technology, systems learning, and individualized self-paced instruction have interfered with successful transfer because the emphasis is on atomized rather than context learning. Many hi-tech instructional packages do not include the opportunity for participants to continuously share what they are learning with others in the program. This opportunity for social transmission during the training process may increase the likelihood of transfer (Ehrenberg 1983, 83).

Maintenance of Behavior

Employees may be motivated to learn new skills, but it requires much greater motivation to alter their behavior. Employees must be able and willing not only to bring their newly learned skills back to the workplace but to apply those skills over a prolonged period until they become routine.

Even when employees are initially enthusiastic about applying new skills, a number of inherent forces usually prevent them from doing so. The most significant factors impeding transfer are related to the organizational climate. They include a lack of on-the-job-reinforcement of new skills, a lack of necessary resources, an absence of managerial interest, and the power of the status quo. Higher-level skills that involve interaction with others are especially vulnerable to social deterrents. Co-workers who did not take the training may be suspicious of any new behavior and react negatively. New supervisory skills can be difficult to apply, particularly when they are different from those used by upper-level management. We tend to supervise as we are supervised, not as we are taught to supervise (Mosel 1957, 62).

In addition to the organizational climate, the employee's abilities and attitudes will affect the degree of transfer. Trainees will be motivated to transfer new skills if they have mastered the content and are aware of the appropriate circumstances in which to apply the new skills. They must perceive that job-performance improvement will likely result, and they must believe that these new skills will be helpful in solving work problems. A trainee's motivation may be influenced by his or her degree of job involvement. Individuals who are deeply involved in their work are more likely to apply new skills, because improved job performance is a significant source of self-esteem (Noe 1986, 742–43). A trainee's "locus-of-control" will also have an effect on the motivation to learn and apply new skills. Those with an internal locus-of-control believe that job performance is contingent on their own behavior and is, therefore, within their control. For this reason, these individuals may exert greater effort in collecting information and attempting new procedures (Noe 1986, 739).

Training is a process, not an episode. To make sure that skills successfully transfer may require a series of meetings between trainer and trainee. Follow-up sessions should be designed to help participants refine their skills and to encourage continued practice. Participants should have a plan specifying when and how they intend to use their new skills. They should be prepared to document the results in a progress report which can be forwarded to the supervisor. Discussion groups can be set up within the organization to help reinforce new behavior.

For training programs to be cost-effective, management support and interest in the program must continue throughout the process. Without positive recognition from the supervisor, the benefits associated with change may appear uncertain, and it may be difficult for the individual to see sufficient intrinsic reward to sustain the new behavior.

While external sources of positive feedback are important, some experts claim that skill retention is largely a self-managed effort (Marx 1986, 55). Any new behavior is susceptible to relapse, and trainees must be aware of this tendency and learn to cope with it. Current relapse-prevention theory is derived from research on addicts that has shown the unfortunate consequences of a single lapse in behavior. Relapse prevention emphasizes gradual improvement. If employees expect to see immediate results, then slow progress may convince them that they are unable to make the changes (Marx 1982, 438). Without relapse-prevention training, a temporary lapse may be seen as a total failure. The employee may attribute this failure to personal inadequacy rather than lack of skills, and the old, less-effective routines will seem preferable (Marx 1982, 436). Relapse-prevention training focuses on the identification of high-risk situations. For example, a circulation clerk attends a training session on dealing calmly with angry patrons. She is able to practice her new skills successfully when she feels confident. She should be aware, however, that certain high-risk situations, such as criticism from her supervisor, may make her overly sensitive to a patron's complaints.

Goal setting is another important posttraining strategy designed to maintain behavior. Goals, especially those that are made publicly, will increase the trainee's commitment to making the necessary changes. Self-managed techniques, such as goal setting and relapse prevention, are important to include in any training program because external sources of reinforcement may be absent or unpredictable.

Conclusion

Transfer is a fundamental but often neglected aspect of training. If new skills fail to transfer to the workplace, then the time and money spent on teaching them has been wasted. When funding is tight, training and staff-development programs will be the first to be cut if management has not seen tangible results. Since cost-benefit analysis is becoming more pervasive and necessary, staff-development efforts must focus on the results, not just the process. The extra effort to ensure the positive transfer of a single skill is worth more than attempts to teach several skills that will be forgotten or discarded.

References

Ehrenberg, Lyle M. "How to Ensure Better Transfer of Learning." *Training and Development Journal* 37 (February 1983): 81–83.

Kelley, Ann I., Robert F. Orgel, and Donald M. Baer. "Seven Strategies That Guarantee Training Transfer." *Training and Development Journal* 39 (November 1985): 78–82.

Leifer, Mellissa S., and John W. Newstrom. "Solving the Transfer of Training Problem." *Training and Development Journal* 34 (August 1980): 42–46.

Marx, Robert D. "Relapse Prevention for Managerial Training: A Model for Maintenance of Behavior Change." *Academy of Management Journal* 7 (June 1982): 433–41.

Marx, Robert D. "Self-Managed Skill Retention." *Training and Development Journal* 40 (January 1986): 54–57.

Mosel, James N. "Why Training Programs Fail to Carry Over." *Personnel* 34 (November–December 1957): 56–64.

Newstrom, John W. "Leveraging Management Development Through the Management of Transfer." *Journal of Management Development* 5, no. 5 (1986): 33–45.

Noe, Raymond A. "Trainees' Attributes and Attitudes: Neglected Influences on Training Effectiveness." *Academy of Management Review* 11, no. 4 (1986): 736–49.

Schendel, Joel D., and Joseph D. Hagman. "On Sustaining Procedural Skills over a Prolonged Retention Interval." *Journal of Applied Psychology* 67 (October 1982): 605–10.

Trost, Arty. "They May Love It but Will They Use It?" *Training and Development Journal* 39 (January 1985): 78–81.

Wexley, Kenneth, and Timothy Baldwin. "Posttraining Strategies for Facilitating Positive Transfer: An Empirical Exploration." *Academy of Management Journal* 29 (September 1986): 503–20.

3 The Place of Training in the Process of Change

Pat L. Weaver-Meyers

Library administrators, managers, and trainers need to work together to ensure that staff-development programs include strategies that facilitate change. Training programs which encourage flexibility and adaptation are as critical as supervisory training. Librarians must learn to manage change as effectively as they manage people.

The process of change has been the subject of much discussion and research in the last twenty years. This research has revealed that certain strategies for planning and implementing change are more successful than others. Successful strategies include involving staff in the planning process, targeting opinion leaders, and informing staff of desired and undesired outcomes (Fine 1986). Training programs which apply these strategies are more likely to produce well-trained staff who support and actively use a new technology or procedure. Without incorporating these strategies into training programs, libraries will be less able to cope with the new demands and developments that are transforming our work.

Training for Change

Understanding why staff accept change is an essential component of the training process. Research on the process of change can tell us which characteristics of individuals, ideas, and organizations lead to accommodation of change and to innovation and which factors produce resistance. For example, Everett M. Rogers (1983, 258) indicates that individuals with well-developed interpersonal communication skills are more likely to adopt innovation. Individuals who are fearful of the negative consequences of change will certainly be more resistant.

In her study on change-agent characteristics of library professionals, Jo Anne A. Hall (1984) concludes that libraries should supply information on the change process in their staff-development programs and help librarians identify and assume the roles of change agents. According to Hall's recommendations, a staff-development officer can stimulate change by developing programs which teach personal networking skills and which include some role-playing sessions on change agentry. Staff who are aware of their own potential to effect change and who are familiar with strategies for winning acceptance for new ideas and procedures will be able to play an active role in the process of change.

Other research on the process of change indicates that a new idea will have a greater chance of being accepted if it is easily adapted, compatible with existing procedures, and has a demonstrable advantage over other solutions (Rogers 1983, 213–31). Training sessions should stress these factors. For example, a typical training program for a new automated circulation system might include the following procedures: charge, discharge, renewal, fines, and holds. A change-oriented agenda would cover the same general procedures but might begin with a presentation on the advantages of automation and conclude with a brainstorming session on adapting existing processes to the new technology.

Rogers also observes that innovative change can sometimes begin with the awareness of a solution, which is then matched with an existing organizational problem (Rogers 1983, 213–31). Rogers calls this phenomenon "scanning for innovation." Adaptive and flexible organizations are regularly scanning the environment for creative and new approaches and ideas. A change-oriented staff-development program should encourage employees to scan for innovation. Routing current journals, fostering attendance at professional meetings, providing access to electronic mail and other discussion forums, and planning brainstorming sessions after conferences are some of the ways in which staff-development personnel can coordinate innovation scanning and problem solving in the library.

Staff-development officers play an important role in promoting organizational growth and development by promoting change in their training programs. They can help staff understand and become more comfortable with the change process by emphasizing the advantages of change to the organization as well as the individual. They can also help staff to take a direct part in creating change by encouraging them to look for new ideas, approaches, and services in the literature and in discussions with colleagues. These strategies are just a few examples of how positive change can be the focus of training sessions.

Role Modeling and Change Agentry

Adequate training is one way to enhance an employee's talent and ability to cope with rapid change. However, a welcoming climate and individuals who initiate and promote change are necessary as well. Thomas W. Shaughnessy (1988) and others share the opinion that organizational climate in libraries may have a greater effect on proposed change than some managers might think. Organizational climate is controlled by many factors, including the library's staff-development program. New employees develop their sense of the library based on interaction with others and on orientation sessions. The focus of introductory training, as well as the emphasis placed on staff development, typifies what is important in a particular library. The structure of the staff-development programs is a signpost to new employees advising them of the possible rewards and penalties associated with innovative behavior. In addition, it is particularly important that staff-development officers and trainers practice the change strategies they preach. Trainers and staff developers themselves should be comfortable with change and should regularly place themselves in the role of change agent. They should be "movers and shakers" or, at very least, be able to recognize and encourage the "movers and shakers" in their library.

What distinguishes a change-receptive staff-development program from a more traditional staff-development effort? Charles R. Martell (1983, 63) suggests that staff development in a dynamic environment should include "elements of autonomy, self-regulation and discretionary decision making." Literature on the process of change uniformly supports staff participation in decision making to help encourage a widespread sense of ownership and commitment. A change-structured staff-development program should emphasize self-directed performance goals explicitly related to change priorities. As an employee progresses, development personnel should shift from being a program trainer to a facilitator, providing resources for self-directed learning.

How do these theories and strategies relate to the creation of a new presentation or workshop? The theory of change suggests that staff should be part of deciding what the program topic should be. Staff should also take part in investigating alternative opportunities for obtaining the same information. In addition, the theory of successful change suggests that programs might best be created by employees with the assistance of staff developers, rather than the other way around. Increasing staff responsibility for their own professional development and rewarding staff for implementing innovative concepts are important components of a change-oriented staff-development program.

What does a change agent do and how can a trainer be an agent of change? In defining some of the roles of a change agent, Ronald G. Havelock (1973) stresses that a change agent works to establish a healthy relationship with employees in which expectations are realistic, both parties are willing to negotiate and compromise when necessary, and communication is adequate and open. As a catalyst for change, the trainer works toward promoting a common purpose, is sensitive to opportunities for change, and implements new procedures when staff seem most receptive to change. For example, there are at least two ways to train staff on a new software package. The trainer can simply present a step-by-step rundown of the procedures and the basic mechanics. However, a trainer who wants to ensure that staff will use the new software might solicit testimonials from other librarians, determine which department would benefit the most and train them first, and schedule the training session when there are apt to be few disruptions and distractions. In other words, the staff developer becomes more than a trainer—the staff developer becomes a promoter or a catalyst for change.

Another role mentioned by Havelock is that of the resource linker. A trainer acting as a resource linker assists employees in their pursuit of additional knowledge. In this example, the trainer may provide the names of software experts, identify relevant reading materials, and help the employee to build personal networks inside and outside the library.

Conclusion

This chapter has briefly outlined a few research findings and strategies associated with planned change. A wealth of published material is available which can help library administrators and trainers to effect positive change within their organizations and help employees cope with and accept new ideas. The following steps will enable staff-development officers and others responsible for personnel training to improve the quality of their programs and increase the chances for successful results.

1. Broaden your own expertise and understanding of the principles of change theory and research.
2. Incorporate change strategies into regular training programs. Stress the advantages of the new procedure and the personal benefits of adapting to change.
3. Organize programs that focus on the change process and on how the individual participant can be an agent of change.
4. Provide programs which develop change-receptive characteristics in the individual, such as personal networking.
5. Include change strategy in your staff-development planning. Encourage staff to participate in the program planning process.
6. Be a role model. Become a promoter, not just a trainer.

References

Baker, Sharon L. "Managing Resistance to Change." *Library Trends* 38 (Summer 1989): 53–61.

Fine, Sara F. "Technological Innovation, Diffusion and Resistance: An Historical Perspective." *Journal of Library Administration* 7 (Spring 1986): 83–108.

Hall, Jo Anne A. "The Relationship between Innovative or Change Agent Characteristics of Librarians in Selected Academic Libraries in the Southeastern United States." Ph.D. diss., University of Michigan, 1984.

Havelock, Ronald G. *The Change Agent's Guide to Innovation in Education.* Englewood Cliffs, N.J.: Educational Technology Publications, 1973.

Martell, Charles R., Jr. *The Client-Centered Academic Library: An Organizational Model.* Westport, Conn.: Greenwood Press, 1983.

Rogers, Everett M. *Diffusion of Innovations.* 3d ed. New York: Free Press, 1983.

Shaughnessy, Thomas W. "Organization Culture in Libraries: Some Management Perspectives." *Journal of Library Administration* 9 (Fall 1988): 5–10.

4

Assessing Training Needs

John Cochenour

A needs assessment establishes a definition of existing training needs. As the first step in the training process, the needs assessment helps to determine what training programs will be most appropriate and effective. When a trainer conducts a needs assessment, the purpose is to develop sufficient information to build an accurate and comprehensive representation of a problem or deficiency which may be solved by adequate training (Gick 1986).

Three Perspectives

For any existing training need or deficiency, three perspectives can be considered: the individual perspective (that of the trainer or trainee), the perspective of the operational unit, and the perspective of the library as a whole. Each typically relates to the perceived benefits or losses associated with a particular solution. Benefits and losses can affect the individual, the unit, and the entire organization (Datta 1978). Training involves change, and change often represents a combination of gains and losses, although a gain for one individual or operational unit does not necessarily mean a gain for another.

The trainer who conducts a needs assessment should examine each possible perspective for two reasons. First, it is important to determine the perspective or view of the problem that is most appropriate for the situation. Second, the trainer must confirm that training is the most effective means of resolving the problem. These two requirements may appear obvious to the reader, but they can be easily overlooked when staff-development plans are being discussed. It is important to remember that not every performance problem can be solved through additional training and staff development.

During the needs-assessment process, the perspective provided by the individual is often related to personal concerns, such as lack of job satisfaction or frustration over ambiguous performance evaluations. A needs assessment which considers the individual perspective might uncover problems such as burnout and fatigue among several employees. The appropriate solutions in this case may focus on adjusted work loads or additional staff rather than on new training programs.

The perspective of the operational unit will be focused primarily on maximum efficiency and will be less concerned with individual needs. This broader perspective often addresses critical issues that individual members within the operational unit might ignore. The needs assessment which takes this perspective might generate solutions that address, for example, inadequate skill levels or a lack of motivation among staff members.

The needs assessment which takes the library's perspective will be the broadest in scope. It might focus on budgetary concerns, comprehensive staff-development programs, and deficiencies that are widespread among operational units. Solutions based on this perspective might reflect the general goals of the parent institution—such as the goals of a university administration.

Models of Needs Assessments

In addition to examining needs from different perspectives, the trainer may adopt several other assessment approaches. Floyd C. Pennington (1980) identified six clusters of needs-assessment models, which vary in scope, purpose, and effectiveness.

System-Discrepancy Model. This is the most common needs-assessment approach. It attempts to measure the difference between the current situation and some optimum level of performance and service by analyzing the gap between actual skills or knowledge and desired skills or knowledge. The problems with this approach stem from the difficulty of defining precisely what the optimum situation should be (Scriven and Roth 1978).

Self-fulfillment. This is a market-strategy approach that targets the interests or wants of a specified group and then presents training opportunities that cater to those interests. Despite its label, one weakness of this approach is that it ignores individual learning needs and skill development and addresses only common preferences.

Individual Appraisal. Unlike the self-fulfillment model, this approach encourages the individual to determine his or her own learning needs. Its major weakness is the difficulty that many people have in honestly assessing their own weaknesses and inabilities.

Diagnostic. This approach defines a need as a harmful deficiency or organizational illness. It discusses needs assessment in terms of general-performance deficits and treatments. A weakness of this model is the difficulty that many organizations have in translating broad prescriptions into feasible actions.

Analytic. This model focuses upon linear problem solving and continued improvement rather than on a one-time remediation. It may be difficult to apply because of the level of abstraction and advanced problem-solving skill required to outline a complex series of actions.

Democratic. This model stresses interactional group efforts in the determination of needs. Unfortunately, the need to reach a consensus may result in an imprecise analysis of critical issues, and the process can be very time consuming.

Regardless of the needs-assessment model selected, the perspective will determine how the problem is defined and what, if any, training programs are employed. Although the models vary in scope and method, the needs-assessment process will include a few basic components which apply to all models.

Components of a Needs Assessment

Judith Fidler and David R. Loughran (1980) define three major steps in the needs-assessment process: a thorough identification of the problem, a classification of the probable causes of the problem, and the generation of possible solutions. The system-discrepancy model can be used to illustrate these steps.

The first step involves identifying and describing specific, observable performances and comparing the existing situation with some operational standard. For example, existing interlibrary loan (ILL) statistics can be compared with an operational standard. This standard might specify that a certain number of ILL requests are reviewed and processed in one hour at 95 percent accuracy.

The second step involves classifying the causes of any discrepancy between the present level of performance and the intended goal. A performance discrepancy can be caused by lack of skills, an environmental disturbance, or insufficient employee motivation and incentive. By classifying the problem, those discrepancies that can be solved through training can be readily identified. The purpose of this phase is to ensure that training efforts are not wasted on problems that require a different approach.

The third step in needs assessment, according to Fidler and Loughran, is the generation of possible solutions based on the information gathered in the first two steps and the selection of the one that is most cost-beneficial. Making this step the final phase of the planning process will guard against our natural tendency to determine solutions before the problem is fully understood. A prepackaged training program or workshop may sound appealing to the personnel librarian or staff-development officer, but much of the effort and cost needed to provide this training will be wasted if the solution does not fulfill a predetermined need. The tendency to be solution or action oriented can result in the "ready-fire-aim" syndrome, which rarely produces the desired outcomes (Hobbs 1990).

Conclusion

By using a needs assessment, the trainer can identify performance gaps and specific training needs. The interpretation of any needs assessment and the design of training programs will be influenced by the perspective selected by the trainer. The perspective can represent the focus of the individual, the unit, or the entire organization. The way a problem is represented will determine the way it is solved, and the method used in analyzing assessment data will affect the way this information is used.

The ultimate goal is to identify the skills and performance levels the staff needs to satisfactorily perform their jobs. There should be a direct relationship among required skills and job knowledge, training programs, and on-the-job-performance (Overfield 1989). Training that is based on clearly identified needs is more likely to produce the desired results, which, in turn, is an effective use of resources.

References

Datta, Lois-Ellin. "Front-End Analysis: Pegasus or Shank's Mare?" *New Directions for Program Evaluation* 1 (Spring 1978): 13–30.

Fidler, Judith, and David R. Loughran. "A Systems Approach." *New Directions for Continuing Education* 7 (1980): 51–64.

Gick, Mary L. "Problem-Solving Strategies." *Educational Psychologist* 21 (1986): 99–120.

Hobbs, David L. "A Training-Appropriations Process." *Training and Development Journal* (May 1990): 109–15.

Overfield, Karen. "Program Development for the Real World." *Training and Development Journal* (Nov. 1989): 66–71.

Pennington, Floyd C. "Needs Assessment: Concepts, Models, and Characteristics." *New Directions for Continuing Education* 7 (1980): 1–14.

Scriven, Michael, and Jane Roth. "Needs Assessment: Concept and Practice." *New Directions for Program Evaluation* 1 (Spring 1978): 1–11.

5 Design of Instructional Programs: Creating Effective Training

Pat L. Weaver-Meyers

As librarians, many, if not most of us are charged with staff-development responsibilities at some time during our careers. Whether presenting a program or workshop to staff, training a new employee, or developing orientation materials, we often do not appreciate fully the complexity of these responsibilities. In developing programs, we usually see our task as one of determining the content of a presentation or preparing training materials but neglect to consider effective implementation strategies. For example, what is the best way to present the information? Will the content be understood more easily and retained longer if the employee sees a videotape, completes a workbook, or listens to a presentation? In what sequence should new information be presented? What should we teach the new employee first—how to search a book order or how to process a vendor list? Does it matter?

Strategies for organizing and presenting training programs fall under the broad heading of instructional design. Familiarity with the instructional-design process can help us evaluate consultant presentations and commercial programs as well as assist us in improving our own training programs. This chapter is intended as a basic introduction for librarians with little or no previous experience in instructional design.

Instructional Design

Instructional Design (ID) is a method of creating training strategies and materials that are both interesting and effective. The ID process helps to ensure that expectations will be clearly stated and understood by both the trainer and the learner. ID theorists believe that the order and way in which we present information has a definite impact on a program's effectiveness. Many institutions employ instructional designers, who help decide the best strategies for a particular presentation or training assignment.

ID theory recommends that a trainer follow a series of nine steps when putting together training programs. These steps are: needs analysis, task description, task analysis, writing objectives, developing tests, formulating instructional strategies, sequencing, developing materials, and preparing formative or summative evaluations (Gropper and Ross 1987). Most trainers are familiar with some of these steps. The most successful programs will include most, if not all, of them.

Step 1. Needs Analysis

The purpose of needs analysis is to determine a goal, describe the current situation, and decide whether staff development can correct an identified inadequacy. Without needs analysis, an excellent training effort may be misdirected and accomplish little. For example, Jane, the head of the circulation department, recently came to the library staff-development committee and requested a presentation on time management to help staff improve their productivity. A needs-analysis interview with the staff, however, revealed that efficiency problems were actually related to the staff's underutilization of the circulation system's software. In this situation, a presentation on time management might be interesting but would not solve Jane's problem.

There are many methods for assessing needs: observing employees in the work environment, interviewing staff, or analyzing performance data are just a few. A more elaborate description of the needs-assessment process has been outlined in the previous chapter. The most critical point to remember when assessing needs is that staff training is not always the most appropriate solution to an identified problem.

Step 2. Task Description

Task description is more appropriate for job-training programs than for general presentations. Task description requires the trainer to identify the steps needed to perform a particular task or job and to determine the best order of execution of these steps. Instructional designers have identified three classes of tasks: action, cognitive, and creative (Davis, Alexander, and Yelon 1974). An action task is readily analyzed and sequenced because all the components can be observed. A cognitive task, which involves perception and knowledge, may require explanation by a learning theorist. A creative task may be difficult for even the expert to describe.

Checking out a book is a typical action task. The task description includes a sequence of actions performed to complete the exchange. Selecting the best source to answer a reference question is an example of a cognitive task. The task description for this procedure would look like a flowchart, representing each step of the decision-making process. Answering an unusually difficult reference request, however, might require a more creative, variable approach. In this case, the task would be difficult, if not impossible, to describe. The kind of task (action, cognitive, or creative) determines what kind of training method will be the most effective.

Step 3. Task Analysis

Robert M. Gagne (1985) assumed that identifiable subskills are necessary before a trainee can learn a new skill. A word-processing trainee, for example, needs to know how to operate a basic keyboard, or should be trained to do so, before learning to use word-processing software. Task analysis clarifies the participant's existing level of knowledge and abilities in relation to the targeted skill level. In other words, the trainer should first confirm that the trainees possess all the prerequisite knowledge to understand the presentation. A program designed to teach the application of several management theories, for example, would require that participants have some knowledge of the theoretical framework on which these applications are based. Requiring participants to read some descriptive material before attending such a session would help to ensure that the participants have the prerequisite level of knowledge to understand the program.

Step 4. Writing Objectives

Once tasks are analyzed, the trainer or manager should formulate objectives based on the type of mental activity required to learn the new skill. Gagne's definition of learning outcomes—verbal information, intellectual skill, cognitive strategy, attitude, or motor skill—represents different levels of performance. For example, memorizing a series of definitions is one level of skill, while solving a problem in a creative way requires different capabilities. Classifying the required type of learning improves the likelihood that the objectives will accurately reflect the expectations.

Written objectives should include action verbs such as "describe," "solve," or "list." The objectives should mention constraints or environmental factors which might impede progress, and should specify measurable results. Below are two examples of written objectives. In Example 1 the results can be measured by assigning the learner the task and determining if it was completed correctly. Example 2 is vague and fails to specify precisely what is expected of the learner.

> Example 1. Given a typical patron request, the learner will be able to create an interlibrary work form in ten minutes on OCLC's interlibrary loan subsystem. One hundred percent accuracy is required for the action to be considered successful.
> Example 2. The learner will become familiar with the OCLC interlibrary loan subsystem.

Step 5. Developing Tests

Testing the trainee can provide useful information to the trainer concerning the effectiveness of the program and help the trainee to measure his or her level of accomplishment. A good test has several features: validity, objectivity, differentiality, and reliability (Davis, Alexander, and Yelon 1974). A test is valid if it requires the learner to perform the same action or skill needed to perform the actual task. A test can be considered objective if it measures the results stated in the task's objectives. A test is differential if it distinguishes between learners who can complete the objectives and learners who cannot. Finally, a test may be considered reliable if it consistently confirms that the learner can complete the assignment.

Pretests can reveal whether the learner possesses the prerequisite skills and can identify learners who may already possess the necessary expertise before training. The results of pretests can be compared with those of posttests to determine the achieved level of learning.

Without testing, objective evaluation is almost impossible. Testing does not have to be in the form of a written examination. Rather, it can take the form of a hands-on demonstration, successful completion of assigned tasks, or verbal reply to case-study presentations. Whatever format is used, correct test design must be based on the stated objectives. In Example 1 under Step 4 above, the best test would determine the level of accuracy and the time it took to complete the interlibrary loan work form.

Step 6. Formulating Instructional Strategies

Instructional strategies should be based on the type of skill required to complete the new task or assignment. Skills generally fall into three categories: cognitive, attitudinal, or motor. Cognitive skills, which involve knowledge and perception, might successfully be taught using traditional classroom techniques, such as lecturing, reading, and discussion. An attitudinal skill, such as a helpful public-service demeanor, might best be taught by role-playing activities rather than a lecture. Motor skills, such as using the computer, usually are taught more effectively by hands-on instruction than by reading a text.

Step 7. Sequencing

Once the general model of instruction is selected, the trainer must determine the appropriate sequence in which to present new concepts. One sequencing approach defined by Gagne includes the following steps: gaining the learner's attention; stimulating recall of prerequisite material; presenting a stimulus; providing guidance; and encouraging performance, feedback, assessment, and retention (Gagne and Driscoll 1988). A trainer who varies the instructional model and sequence according to the type and level of required learning will be more successful than the trainer who sticks to a single formula.

Step 8: Developing Materials

Once the general strategy is determined, the trainer needs to design or select appropriate and effective teaching materials. Researchers have determined that certain learning traits, such as aptitude, anxiety level, spatial ability, mastery of study skills, and motivation, can alter the impact of certain training materials (Tobias 1987). Libraries faced with limited time and resources may find it difficult to conduct a thorough analysis of these traits. At very least, material design should take into account the type of skill required—attitudinal, cognitive, or motor.

Step 9: Formative or Summative Evaluation

Two types of evaluation, formative and summative, are part of the design process. Formative evaluation, which is used less often because of time constraints, involves testing the training program initially on a small group, then revising it if necessary before it is implemented on a wider scale.

Summative evaluation, which is used more frequently, examines whether the training's objectives are worthwhile, identifies unexpected outcomes not specified in the objectives, and compares the outcome with standardized test results. Brief surveys which ask participants to rate the presentation sometimes fall short of a complete summative evaluation. According to Leslie J. Briggs (1977), summative evaluations should also measure the likelihood of trainees to use the materials in real situations and compare costs of different training methods. Ideally, the summative evaluation is completed by an independent evaluator.

Conclusion

Instructional design is a systematic process used to create training programs and materials. Instructional designers recognize the complexity of the learning process and the importance of matching needs with appropriate and effective programs. For librarians confronted with the challenge of designing their own programs and training materials, ID can provide a structured technique for defining and organizing staff-development needs. This brief discussion provides a general theoretical background intended to help the reader understand the practical discussions on methodology in later chapters.

References

Briggs, Leslie J. "Introduction." In *Instructional Design,* edited by Leslie J. Briggs. Englewood Cliffs, N.J.: Educational Technology Publications, 1977.

Davis, Robert H., Lawrence T. Alexander, and Stephen L. Yelon. *Learning System Design: An Approach to the Improvement of Instruction.* New York: McGraw-Hill, 1974.

Gagne, Robert M. *The Conditions of Learning and Theory of Instruction,* 4th ed. New York: Holt, Rinehart and Winston, 1985.

Gagne, Robert M., and Marcy Perkins Driscoll. *Essentials of Learning for Instruction.* Englewood Cliffs, N.J.: Prentice-Hall, 1988.

Gropper, George L., and Paul A. Ross. "Instructional Design." In *Training and Development Handbook: A Guide to Human Resource Development,* 3d ed., edited by Robert L. Craig. New York: McGraw-Hill, 1987.

Tobias, Stephen. "Learner Characteristics." In *Instructional Technology: Foundations,* edited by Robert M. Gagne. Hillsdale, N.J.: Lawrence Erlbaum Associates, 1987.

PART II   METHODS

P L A N N I N G

---

6   How to Get Started: Questions to Ask Yourself

Anne Grodzins Lipow

There are two wonderful attributes inherent in staff development: the initiative for it can come from anyone anywhere in the organization, and the object of it is human growth. Whether that initiative blossoms or withers and whether staff members grow or stagnate depend on how thoughtfully the process toward fulfillment is managed. The questions in this chapter are intended to ensure a thoughtful consideration of the range of issues pertinent to a beginning staff development effort. There are no right or wrong answers to these questions except as they relate to your specific undertaking.

Think Small: The One-Shot Program

1. Is there a particular **program/issue** of interest to a significant segment of your staff? If no, why do you want a staff-development program? (Maybe something else will address the need.) If yes, which issue(s)? Which staff? How do you know this?
2. What **benefit(s)** should result? Improved staff morale? New knowledge? Improved performance? Changed performance? Increased effectiveness? Cost savings? What results or outcomes are sought? By whom?
3. Who makes up the **target audience**?
4. What **format** is appropriate? Panel discussion with large audience? Workshop with few participants? Film? Single speaker? Seminar? Newsletter? Information-sharing "clinic?" Informal, staff-initiated staff gathering (e.g., bag lunch)? How have others handled the topic?
5. Who should **organize** it? Administrative task force? Existing staff committee? Ad hoc committee of interested staff within one library unit or among library units?
6. How can **administrative support** be obtained when it is lacking?

25

Have the administrative objections been addressed? Have the expected benefits been articulated sufficiently? Is the maximum staff support for the program evident?

7. How much time should be allotted for **preparation**? Allow more time (up to six months) the more of the following that apply: contracting for speaker(s) and agreeing on fees and expenses (if any), program date, room requirements, and equipment; scheduling the room and arranging for the setup of the room and special equipment; preparing (writing and designing) handouts; producing and duplicating handouts; handling publicity, preenrollment, and confirmation of enrollment; arranging for the presence of a technician to handle on-the-spot technical problems or for an assistant to help with furniture moving and other setup activities the day of the program; arranging for refreshments and lunch; preparing name tags, registration sheets, and evaluation form.

8. **Who is eligible** to attend? Participants appointed by administration? Voluntary? Maximum attendance allowed? Minimum attendance required?

9. How should the program be **publicized**? Is program description geared toward the intended audience? Does publicity clearly identify the intended audience?

10. What **facilities and equipment** are needed? Arrangement of room for lecture? For discussion? Flexible seating for interchanging small- and large-group gatherings? Will attendees need writing surfaces? Writing materials? Where to go for breaks? Food? Will speaker's voice carry? Ambience of room: stuffy air? Light enough? Comfortable enough? Can thermostat be adjusted at will? Blackboard? Easels, pens, and masking tape? Projectors (for transparencies, slides, film)? Computer demos? Monitors, modems, phone lines (test them out)? Sufficient electrical outlets?

11. How should the program be **evaluated**? Were expected benefits derived? How do you know? How will you measure the change (in morale, knowledge, behavior, etc.) as a result of the program? Was need fulfilled? Is it worth repeating? What mistakes were made? What was left out? What was done especially well?

12. **What next?** Should a report be written up and distributed? If worth repeating, how often? Should new staff eventually be reached with this program? If yes, how? Is this the start of something bigger—one of a series on a broader topic?

Developing a Continuing Program

1. Is there agreement about a **definition** of staff development? Position-related? Career-related? Primary beneficiary: individual? Library? Must enhance or support library goals? Which ones? Does a written policy exist for your organization?

2. Who is doing what for whom? What and whose **needs** have been identified and assessed? To what extent are these needs already being

met? Is there agreement among staff and between staff and administration about the need? In whole? In part? If no, how can agreement
be reached—in whole or in part? Is there agreement about the
expected outcome?

3. What **types of programs** would fulfill the need(s) and achieve the
   desired outcome(s)? Ones that improve skills? Change behavior?
   Broaden perspectives? Address issues of immediate concern? How do
   they match with definition of staff development?

4. Where to find the **expert speakers and presenters**? Internally?
   From parent organization (e.g., city, state, campus)? From nearby
   library? Regional continuing education programs? Library consultants?
   Recommendations from other libraries? Professional organizations or
   associations—regional, state, national?

5. Do program presenters have not only expertise in the program topic
   but also **skills in making effective presentations**? Can internal
   staff with knowledge of program topic be given training in oral or
   written presentation skills to develop in-house presenters?

6. How to promote **transfer of learning** to on-the-job performance?
   Establish expectations ahead of time with participants' supervisors?
   With participants? With program leaders? Ensure continued learning
   environment on the job (e.g., coaching, practice time)? Plan to follow
   up to check out expectations?

7. **Budget**? Costs? Fees for outside speakers? How much for publicity?
   Refreshments? Facilities rental? Film rental? Handouts? Hidden costs—
   staff time, things not getting done because of this program? Registration fees and travel funding for external workshops? (Remember to
   weigh these costs against costs of *not* doing the program.) What
   sources of funding? Is cost recovery possible—e.g., external sale of
   well-developed program materials or jointly sponsored program with
   nearby library(ies)?

Follow-up

1. Who will be responsible for **continued programming**? Ensuring a
   postprogram on-the-job learning environment until program objectives are reached? Continued assessment of needs? Adherence to
   program standards? Advocating adequate funding? Continued evaluation of programs? An individual? A committee? A combination?

2. To what extent will attendance be **voluntary** versus **mandatory**?

3. How will follow-up planning occur to ensure **skills transfer** after
   each program?

4. Over a one-year period, what **new programs** will be given? What
   programs will be repeated? What programs over a two-year period?

5. Over time, who approves allocation of **funds** for staff development?
   Administration? A balance of administration and staff? How often do
   the individuals who approve funds change?

6. From where and whom are **ideas** for new programs being solicited?
   How?

Examples of Staff-Development Programs

Improve skills/Change performance/Retrain

time management

clear writing (reports, manuals, correspondence, training materials)

job rotation

on-line catalogs (training in, teaching; downloading from)

managing bibliographic files

interviewing techniques at service desks

interviewing techniques for hiring

care of library materials

training new employees

evaluating performance

managing student/temporary employees

designing/redesigning jobs

using microcomputers (to access remote files, download, upload, write reports, keep records)

using statistics

conducting meetings

team building

"first impression" staff

dealing with angry/difficult patrons

handling "disturbed" patrons

writing grant proposals

instruction techniques

computer programming

Broaden perspectives

problems/trends in
    automation
    information storage and retrieval
    conservation

job rotation

new employee orientation

senior employee reorientation

unit-by-unit orientation

working in a multicultural environment

new concepts in
    scholar workstations
    collection nonbook formats (software, microform, etc.)
    library organization

librarian as information consultant

relation of library to
    institution
    community
    end-user searching

Cultivate awareness of today's issues

VDTs/ergonomics

AIDS

illiteracy

budget/fiscal issues

space design

the changing work force

charging for library services

changes in forms and methods of information access

the government's role in dissemination of information

copyright

managing change; dealing with resistance to change

how automation affects library jobs

7 How to Gather Support

Janet T. Paulk

If your library is slow to support staff development, it may need your help in paving the way. Perhaps the administration is unaware of the numerous ways in which staff development can benefit the library—and, perhaps, staff members are unaware of the many ways in which it can benefit them as individuals. Below are a few suggestions which may assist you in helping change the perspectives of management and staff and enable your organization to establish a staff-development program.

Do Your Homework

Read and assess literature concerning staff-development programs and the many kinds of related activities to get a **wide range of ideas.** Select those that are compatible with your library.

Search through your library's annual reports, written goals and objectives, and other **pertinent reports** for statements that might justify or support the concept of staff development.

Identify and **contact other libraries** that have successful staff-development programs. Find out how they got started; ask them about programs that require little or no funding, yet have been effective.

Get on the **mailing list** of libraries with both staff-development programs and newsletters, targeting larger libraries that have a personnel or staff-development officer and state library agencies.

Define Staff Development

What it is not: Staff development is neither continuing education, which is a lifelong process and usually the responsibility of each individual staff member, nor a break from work.

What it is: Staff development is a program which **guides and encourages employees to develop their skills** and capabilities on a continuing basis. The intent is to improve the performance of both the individual and the organization and to maximize staff effectiveness. Staff development serves institutional needs and enhances the ability of the organization to meet its goals. To put it simply, it is an effort to help employees learn how to do their jobs better.

Staff development may or may not include career development. As libraries move in new directions, however, staff-development programs can assist staff in preparing for changes in their present jobs. It also can prepare them to assume new responsibilities within the library.

Examine What Is Being Done Now

Develop a list of what is already being done in your library. Many activities may currently fall under the heading of staff development. A few might include:

Routing professional journals or tables of contents
Performance appraisals
Library orientation
Committee assignments
Staff meetings
Travel opportunities and professional membership activities

Once you begin identifying these efforts as part of "staff development," staff's and management's perceptions of what staff development is will alter.

Talk It Up

Identify key people in your organization who support staff development as a way to assist the organization in carrying out its mission. Talk to them about the value of staff development and get them to talk to others. Teach staff and management to perceive staff development as something that can help them to do their jobs better. Create an informal sales pitch to use in the lunchroom and during breaks.

Identify a few needs. The process is sometimes called *needs assessment*, but at this point it does not have to be formal or lengthy. Try to identify needs in an informal setting—simply ask people what they perceive would help them do their jobs more effectively. (For more on needs assessment, see chapters 4, 8, and 9).

Do What You Can Do

Start a **brown-bag lunch** discussion group with persons who have indicated an interest in staff development. Focus on a different aspect of staff development at each meeting. For example, each person might be responsible for sharing information from an assigned journal; or persons who attend professional meetings or programs might share information about those activities.

Develop a Proposal and Submit It

Get several of the employees who are most interested in staff development to help you develop a proposal for the library's administration. Include in your proposal a list of staff-development activities that are already implemented.

Divide the list into activities that do not require time away from the job and those that do.

Concentrate on activities that speak directly to the goals of the organization.

Points to Include

Request an opportunity to visit other libraries.

Request permission to start a collection of staff-development literature. All you need is a bookcase in the employee lunchroom or lounge. Plan to include newsletters from other libraries and professional journals. If your library does not subscribe to many journals, ask individuals to donate their personal copies.

Suggest starting notebooks for departmental and librarywide annual reports for your library. The notebooks might also include copies of meeting minutes. Develop a plan to notify staff of recent additions to the "staff-development collection."

In your proposal, include the results of your informal needs assessment and request support to conduct a more formal needs assessment in the future.

Indicate how proposed activities can help the organization and individuals do a better job.

Request that a staff-development committee be appointed and that a member of top management be included on the committee.

Plan for Success

When your committee is formed, start with something you can do well. **Go for sure success the first time.** Assess what impact this effort has made. Report to top management on your success. Report to staff on your success. Try to build momentum for further staff support.

When you sense that the time is right—perhaps after the committee has delivered its formal needs assessment to top management or after the first few programs—request that staff-development responsibilities be made an official part of someone's job. To ensure credibility, that person should be an upper-level administrator or someone who is not identified with a single unit or department.

8

How to Identify Staff's Needs

Kenna Forsyth

If you are responsible for your library's staff-development program, keeping your eyes and ears open to staff needs should become second nature. In a climate of openness and trust, the information gathered through conversations and observations should present an accurate picture of staff-development needs. Asking for staff's input will build their interest and commitment to staff-development activities and help you plan more effective programs. Be sure to justify all activities by linking them to your needs assessment.

As mentioned in chapter 4, there are many different ways of conducting a needs assessment. The following chapter, "Designing and Conducting a Needs Assessment," covers the more in-depth, complex assessment processes for the library that is ready to make a major commitment of library resources to staff development. This chapter offers an informal alternative to libraries that want to begin the staff-development effort but may be unequipped to embark on a comprehensive plan. A brief outline of the advantages and disadvantages of a more formal assessment is also included.

Informal Approach

Ask around and get the opinions of supervisors, management groups, and committees as to what kinds of programs are needed.

Listen for phrases that might suggest a need for staff development: "This isn't working very well" or "we could do this better." Be aware of recurring negative experiences that staff may be having, such as the inability to handle conflict. Then pursue the topic, press for details, and ask others to validate the problem.

Look at **performance evaluations.** What deficiencies does the supervisor note? Get feedback from the staff member as to the direction his or her development should take in the next year. Does the employee want to improve current skills or to develop skills to handle new responsibilities.

Support staff members who are new in their jobs. Look at the job description or skills inventory for those jobs. What do staff need to learn that they are not bringing to their jobs?

Examine documents, such as long-range plans, goals and objectives statements, and employee-survey results, for hints on how to bring about improvement.

On all workshop evaluation forms ask: "What other topics for discussion or training would be of benefit to you?"

Establish a **staff-development committee** to help you collect and analyze data.

Formal Approach

There are three primary methods of gathering data: the questionnaire (open-ended or forced choice), the one-on-one interview (in person or by phone), and the group interview (either structured[1] or unstructured[2]).

The Questionnaire

Advantages:

Reaches a large number of
     employees
Protects confidentiality
Requires skill to design

Disadvantages:

Takes time to develop
Responses may be ambiguous and
     hard to interpret

One-on-One Interviews

Advantages:

Encourages free expression
Allows interviewer to clarify
     responses

Disadvantages:

Time consuming
Requires skilled interviewer
Sometimes difficult to analyze data

---

1. A structured group interview is described in *Continuing Education Needs Assessment: A Group Interview Technique* (CLENE Occasional Paper, No. 1), available from the ALA. This publication describes a group-interview technique which identifies topics of interest, continuing-education providers, sources of support, and incentives for participating in continuing-education activities. The topics generated by the group interview can then be used to construct a questionnaire.

2. A relatively unstructured group interview is called a *focus group.* This is a directed discussion with eight to ten individuals. A moderator guides the discussion, using questions that solicit opinions, perceptions, and attitudes about services, issues, and ideas. Discussions are audiotaped so that the moderator can write up the results. For more information, see a report from the Denver Public Library by Suzanne Walters, *Focus Groups: Linkages to the Community;* also contact RIVA Marketing Research and Training Services, 4609 Willow Lane, Chevy Chase, MD 20815.

Group Interviews

Advantages:

Allows for synthesizing different viewpoints

Builds support for staff-development activities

Disadvantages:

Time consuming

Requires skilled interviewer

May be difficult to integrate different viewpoints

9 Designing and Conducting a Needs Assessment

Charles E. Kratz

Successful staff-development programs are relevant to the needs of the staff. A library can determine its staff needs by conducting a needs assessment. As discussed in chapter 4, a needs assessment is the process by which an organization asks its staff what they need to do their jobs better and, from the answers, determines a plan of action. The process may range from a simple survey to a complex investigation. Properly done, a needs assessment can be the foundation upon which a strong staff-development program is built.

The previous chapter, "How to Identify Staff Needs," suggests some easy-to-do, less formal ways of learning what staff needs are. This chapter covers the more in-depth, complex assessment process for the library that is ready to make a major commitment of library resources to staff development. Formal questionnaires should be constructed by someone with expertise to ensure that the questions will yield relevant, usable answers. The follow-up must be timely and commensurate with the expectations raised by the needs-assessment process itself.

At the end of this chapter are examples of needs-assessment questionnaires used by two libraries—the Tacoma Public Library and the University of Michigan Library. Note the way the questions try to reduce ambiguity and evoke clear and measurable responses. Also note that both libraries have a long-standing commitment to staff development and to well-developed, comprehensive staff-development programs.

The Value of a Needs Assessment

A needs assessment can:

- Assist management in planning staff-development activities

- Identify organizational and individual needs and help prioritize those needs
- Identify training needs based on the goals of the organization
- Identify attitudes concerning new services, skills, or technologies
- Identify future opportunities for the organization
- Identify performance gaps, i.e., when an individual's work performance does not meet expectations
- Determine the cause of certain performance problems and identify possible solutions
- Determine whether a need is the result of a training problem, such as a skills deficit, or a nontraining issue, such as policy clarification
- Provide a checklist of needs for trainers

The Process

A. Preparing for the Needs Assessment
   1. Determine **who** will be responsible for conducting the needs assessment.
   2. Obtain **management support**. This may be the single most important step in the preparation for a needs assessment. It sends the message to the staff that you are serious about wanting the program to be responsive to their needs.
   3. Obtain **employee support**. Emphasize the positive outcomes. Without employee support, the response you receive may not be completely candid.
   4. Determine if an **external consultant** is needed for any phase of the assessment.
   5. Gather **background information**. Search through documentation from previous assessments that measure competence, and deficiency in service. Look at the organization's goals and objectives. Seek out information concerning change and its impact on the organization. Identify past attempts to improve operations, programs, and services.
   6. Identify **expenses,** including the staff time spent on planning, preparation, and implementation and the cost of materials, supplies, and printing.
   7. Identify **people** on your staff who can help move the process forward—those with an understanding of the problem(s), experience in training, and knowledge of available funds.
   8. Identify **constraints**—time, cost, political, and personnel—that might hinder the process.
B. Defining the Goals and Objectives of the Needs Assessment
   1. Define the **purpose and scope** of the assessment, the aspects to be analyzed, and the expected outcome.
   2. Relate this effort to the overall goals of the organization.
C. Conducting the Needs Assessment
   1. Examine data collected prior to the assessment, such as attitude

surveys, job descriptions, performance appraisals, work samples, and performance standards.

2. Identify what new **data** are needed; identify specific questions that need to be answered.
3. Determine the **best time** to conduct an assessment and how long it will take to complete.
4. Design an effective **data-gathering method** for your organization. Use questionnaires and surveys, interviews, observations, reviews of written resources, task and competency surveys, focus groups, assessment centers, informal discussions, and advisory committees. Design an approach or method for gathering data from employees at different levels of the organization.
5. Determine if the assessment will be administered by in-house or external sources.
6. Identify the population—what department and which employees will be involved in the process.
7. Identify the **budgeted amount** available to cover costs incurred in the process.
8. Consider various **sampling strategies**. Before any approach is used on the entire staff, it is a good idea to test it with a sample group.
9. Listen carefully, avoid personal **bias**, and emphasize **accuracy** in gathering data.
10. Determine whether the information collected will remain **confidential**.

D. Analyzing and Verifying the Data
1. **Verify** the content of the documentation, identifying any inconsistent responses.
2. Analyze the gathered information to determine **priorities** for training and program planning.
3. Distinguish between training and nontraining problems.

E. Presenting the Conclusions and Recommendations
1. Design possible solutions for the identified needs, problems, and issues.
2. Determine which solutions are cost effective.
3. Put results, conclusions, and recommendations into written form and present them to the library administration.
4. Report results to the staff.

F. Implementing Recommended Solutions to Enhance Organizational or Individual Effectiveness

Implementation is important for credibility; the organization must act in accordance with the expectations raised by the assessment process. If no action is taken, staff morale may be adversely affected.
1. Develop and implement plans for training activities and programs that address the priority needs, problems, and issues.
2. Do not waste time. Plan at least one event to take place soon after the assessment has been analyzed.

3. Plan for **follow-up** after each program to ensure that skills learned in a training session are practiced on the job.

G. Evaluate How Effectively the Needs Assessment Met Its Objectives

1. Ask people if they thought the needs assessment was **thorough and on target.**

2. Develop a method for **evaluating the results** of training programs and staff-development activities. Make sure that the evaluation process will yield candid information. Make sure that this process is feasible. (See chapter 17.)

3. Analyze the results. Do the results address the goals and objectives defined earlier?

4. Be prepared to respond to negative evaluations. Have a **contingency plan.** Know what to do in case the training efforts have failed to produce the desired results. Be prepared to respond to expressed needs for further staff-development activities.

H. Maintaining the Needs Assessment Process as a Continuing Part of the Staff-Development Program

1. Establish a **continuing schedule** for the needs-assessment process. Determine how often the assessment should be done and who will be responsible for its implementation.

2. Consider **varying** the data-gathering approach or method.

3. Be **alert** to changing goals and objectives.

Examples of Needs-Assessment Questionnaires

The Tacoma Public Library

To: All Staff
From: Michael Taft
Personnel/Labor Relations Officer
Subject: TPL—Training/Staff

Date: 17 July 1984

Development Survey

The Library is seeking information from all regular full-time and part-time staff to assist in planning staff development activities. This questionnaire is based on the following definitions. Staff training/development is defined as:

1. opportunities to expand skills, knowledge and abilities in order to improve work performance and to increase understanding of library functions.
2. opportunities that enable staff to improve all the skills represented in their [employment] class.
3. opportunities that enable staff to become acquainted with skills, knowledge not in their current [employment] class, and
4. programs may be presented in a variety of formats including but not limited to: structured in-house course work, lectures, seminars, team work groups, individual projects, tours, etc.

This questionnaire and the plan that will develop from the information gathered is concerned with your ideas as staff in regards to your training/staff development. Listed on the following pages are some questions developed by the Personnel Office to assist the Library and staff in developing a plan. Please complete the questionnaire and return it to the Personnel Office by July 30, 1984.
Thank you.

Part I

1. Name _____
   (optional)
2. Please check items that apply to your position:
   a. Location
      Main _____
      Public Service _____
      Tech Service _____
      Branches _____
      Administration _____
      Maintenance _____

   b. Classification
      Admin. _____
      Mgmt. _____
      Supvr. _____
      Librarian _____
      Sr. Lib. Assoc. _____
      Lib. Assoc. _____
      Library Aide _____
      Maintenance _____
      Other _____
      Unlisted _____

    c. Length of Employment

       less than 1 year _____

       1-3 years _____

       4-6 years _____

       7-9 years _____

       10-12 years _____

       13-15 years _____

       16 years & over _____

3. Have you held more than one class in your tenure with the Tacoma Public Library (i.e., aide to associate)?

    Yes _____   No _____

4. When you first came to the Tacoma Public Library as a new employee, did you participate in an orientation program for new employees?

    Yes _____   No _____

    a. A work site orientation (trained in areas needed to complete a task, the facets of a job)

       Yes _____   No _____

    b. A job orientation (signed up for various benefit programs, introduced to TPL as an organization, rules/regulations, etc.)

       Yes _____   No _____

5. Was the program listed in #4 adequate for your needs?

    Yes _____   No _____   Uncertain _____

    a. List suggestions for improvement in the orientation program:

    _____

    _____

    _____

    _____

6. Has the training for your position met your needs?

    Yes _____   No _____

    Do you have any suggestions for improving training for your position? If so, please list them:

    _____

    _____

    _____

    _____

7. Does your current position require on-the-job training to keep up with developments that affect your work?

    Yes _____   No _____

    a. What kind of on-the-job training are you currently receiving?

    _____

    _____

    _____

b. Do you have any suggestions for improving on-the-job training?

_____

_____

_____

8. Have you participated in any library sponsored workshops, lectures or in-service training sessions?

Yes _____   No _____

If yes, which ones:

_____

_____

_____

_____

_____

a. Do you believe that these activities were helpful?

Yes _____   No _____

If not, please indicate the reasons:

_____

_____

_____

_____

9. Were training sessions held that might have been useful to you, but you were unable to attend?

Yes _____   No _____

a. If yes, why were you not able to attend?

_____

_____

10. Have you participated in conferences, seminars, workshops or lectures held outside of the Library while you have been employed at TPL which were directly related to your position?

Yes _____   No _____

a. If yes, do you believe that attending these outside programs was worthwhile in helping you meet the needs of your position?

Yes _____   No _____

b. List the programs attended:

_____

_____

_____

_____

11. Can you think of any kind of in-house training or outside training not currently offered that would help you improve your job performance?

    Yes _____   No _____

    a. If yes, please list:

    _____

    _____

    _____

    _____

    _____

Part II

The Personnel Office has identified a number of training/staff development topics that may be of interest. This part of the survey is to find out the number of staff interested in a particular program as well as the level of interest. This list is by no means exhaustive so we welcome comments and suggestions for other programs.

Check your interest level:

	No Interest	Low Interest	Moderate Interest	High Interest
1. Library tours				
a. tours of TPL branches/departments	_____	_____	_____	_____
b. tours of other area libraries	_____	_____	_____	_____
2. Training Sessions by TPL Staff				
a. library terminology	_____	_____	_____	_____
b. using common bibliographic terms	_____	_____	_____	_____
c. circulation policies/procedures	_____	_____	_____	_____
d. interlibrary loan	_____	_____	_____	_____
e. basic reference tools	_____	_____	_____	_____
f. filing rules/use of card catalog	_____	_____	_____	_____
g. acquisition process	_____	_____	_____	_____
h. OCLC training tapes	_____	_____	_____	_____
i. basics of automation	_____	_____	_____	_____
j. government publications	_____	_____	_____	_____
k. intellectual freedom	_____	_____	_____	_____

	No Interest	Low Interest	Moderate Interest	High Interest
l. on-line reference	_____	_____	_____	_____
m. micro computer	_____	_____	_____	_____

3. Training sessions presented by Admin.:

	No Interest	Low Interest	Moderate Interest	High Interest
a. payroll	_____	_____	_____	_____
b. budget	_____	_____	_____	_____
c. personnel procedures	_____	_____	_____	_____
d. insurance	_____	_____	_____	_____
e. safety/security	_____	_____	_____	_____
f. programming	_____	_____	_____	_____
g. admin. operations	_____	_____	_____	_____
h. other	_____	_____	_____	_____

4. Seminars/workshops presented by specialist in:

	No Interest	Low Interest	Moderate Interest	High Interest
a. communication skills	_____	_____	_____	_____
b. mgmt. by objectives	_____	_____	_____	_____
c. copyright law	_____	_____	_____	_____
d. leadership	_____	_____	_____	_____
e. performance appraisal	_____	_____	_____	_____
f. management skills	_____	_____	_____	_____
g. supervisory skills	_____	_____	_____	_____
h. problem employee	_____	_____	_____	_____
i. discipline/discharge	_____	_____	_____	_____
j. public relations	_____	_____	_____	_____
k. effective writing	_____	_____	_____	_____
l. team building	_____	_____	_____	_____

m. grievance handling   _____   _____   _____   _____

n. stress management   _____   _____   _____   _____

o. time management   _____   _____   _____   _____

p. orientation of new employees   _____   _____   _____   _____

q. reorientation of employees   _____   _____   _____   _____

r. EEO/AA plan   _____   _____   _____   _____

s. indexing   _____   _____   _____   _____

t. marketing   _____   _____   _____   _____

u. planning   _____   _____   _____   _____

v. interview techniques   _____   _____   _____   _____

w. organization change   _____   _____   _____   _____

x. patron relations   _____   _____   _____   _____

aa. intellectual freedom   _____   _____   _____   _____

ab. on-line reference   _____   _____   _____   _____

ac. microcomputer   _____   _____   _____   _____

Other

_____

_____

5. Are you interested in job rotation?
   Yes _____   No _____
   a. only within your own department/division _____
   b. between departments with related activities _____
   c. between any library department _____
   d. location to rotate to

   _____

6. Would you like to have training/staff development opportunities?
   a. to aid you in present position _____
   b. to aid you in meeting requirements for future positions _____
   c. other

   _____

7. What kind of staff development programs would be appropriate for library staff?

_____

_____

_____

_____

_____

8. Any other comments concerning training/staff development?

_____

_____

_____

University of Michigan Library
Staff Development Needs-Assessment Questionnaire

Part 1: All Staff

The Staff Development Advisory Committee is seeking information from all library staff to assist in planning staff development activities. This questionnaire is based on the following definition:

The Library has established a Staff Development Program which is broad in scope, including the following three components:

Orientation: Provides employees with introduction to the job and work environment, orientation to the library organization, and orientation to the University.

Training: Provides employees with knowledge and skills necessary to perform their responsibilities effectively.

Development: Provides employees with concepts and general techniques and/or with general background and understanding in order to accept new or increased responsibilities and to respond positively to change.

1. Please check all that apply to your position:
    _____ Divisional Library   _____ Technical Services
    _____ Public Services   _____ Administrative Services
2. Length of employment in UM Library:
    _____ less than 1 year   _____ 1-4 years
    _____ 5-10 years   _____ more than 10 years
3. Job Family:
    _____ clerical   _____ librarian
    _____ P & A   _____ AFSCME
4. Least desirable time for you to attend training sessions:
    least desirable days of week: ___ Monday ___ Tuesday ___ Wednesday ___ Thursday ___ Friday
    least desirable times of day: ___ AM ___ PM
    least desirable months: ___ September ___ October ___ November ___ December ___ January ___ February ___ March ___ April ___ May ___ June ___ July ___ August

Possible Staff Development Programs

(Please circle your interest level for each topic)
(No Interest=0 Low=1 Moderate=2 High=3 No Opinion=4)

Orientation

1. Where would I find 3A in the Graduate Library?
    0   1   2   3   4
2. What should I do in case of a medical emergency or fire?
    0   1   2   3   4
3. What are personnel policies regarding Leave of Absences?
    0   1   2   3   4
4. What are library borrowing privileges for staff?
    0   1   2   3   4

5. When do I receive a paycheck and what period does it cover?

    0   1   2   3   4

6. Where are UM dissertations located?

    0   1   2   3   4

7. What is the policy on flexible schedule?

    0   1   2   3   4

8. What is the Library committee structure and how do I participate?

    0   1   2   3   4

9. How can I find what I want in the card catalog?

    0   1   2   3   4

10. How is a book selected for the Library?

    0   1   2   3   4

11. How is a book acquired and processed?

    0   1   2   3   4

12. How does my work/unit fit into the library picture?

    0   1   2   3   4

13. How can I get to meet other staff outside my own unit who perform similar tasks?

    0   1   2   3   4

14. What is the extent of the materials in divisional libraries represented by the cards in the Graduate Library catalog?

    0   1   2   3   4

15. Where are government documents kept?

    0   1   2   3   4

16. What skills should I try to develop to eventually get a better job in the library system?

    0   1   2   3   4

17. Other Questions/Issues:

    _____

    _____

Communication Skills

18. How can I improve my listening skills?

    0   1   2   3   4

19. How can I improve my ability to explain library services to users?

    0   1   2   3   4

20. What are techniques for dealing with a difficult interaction with a user?

    0   1   2   3   4

21. What are ways to handle the variety of phone questions in an efficient and tactful manner?

    0   1   2   3   4

22. How can I indicate disagreement with someone's ideas without being critical of the person?

    0   1   2   3   4

23. How can I write better reports?

    0   1   2   3   4

24. How can I improve my public speaking skills?

    0   1   2   3   4

25. How can I find out what library terms and jargon really mean? (BRC, incomplete separates, fixed fields, ARL, etc.)

    0   1   2   3   4

26. How can I improve my reference interview skills?
    0   1   2   3   4
27. Other Questions/Issues:

_____

_____

Organizational Skills

28. How can I make the best use of my time?
    0   1   2   3   4
29. How can I learn to set priorities?
    0   1   2   3   4
30. How should I deal with stress in my job?
    0   1   2   3   4
31. How can I assess the impact that my work habits have on my co-workers?
    0   1   2   3   4
32. How should I organize my work to be most efficient?
    0   1   2   3   4
33. Other Questions/Issues:

_____

_____

Automated Systems

(Indicate your interest level in a general overview of each system)
34. GEAC (circulation system)
    0   1   2   3   4
35. INNOVAQ (acquisition system)
    0   1   2   3   4
36. BRS, DIALOG (database searching)
    0   1   2   3   4
37. RLIN (cataloguing and bibliographic system)
    0   1   2   3   4
38. MIRLYN (Integrated Library System)
    0   1   2   3   4
39. MTS (campus electronic message system)
    0   1   2   3   4
40. Microcomputers
    0   1   2   3   4
41. Other Questions/Issues:

_____

_____

Issues in Research Librarianship

42. What are techniques and approaches for collection evaluation?

    0   1   2   3   4

43. What are developments in and implications of materials in electronic format?

    0   1   2   3   4

44. What are the implications for service surrounding the issue of ownership/copyright of bibliographic data bases?

    0   1   2   3   4

45. What is the potential impact of automation on library organizations (jobs, staffing, work process, etc.?)

    0   1   2   3   4

46. How do public service values get translated into activities and programs?

    0   1   2   3   4

47. What new roles might develop for librarians over the next decade?

    0   1   2   3   4

48. How can librarians get more involved in research and publication, and why is this important?

    0   1   2   3   4

49. What are the issues in higher education that will have a direct impact on libraries?

    0   1   2   3   4

50. What are the primary economic issues facing libraries?

    0   1   2   3   4

51. Other Issues/Questions:

_____

_____

Preservation

The following sessions/services are being considered for the next two years.

    (Please circle your interest level for each topic)

1. Simple Repairs

    0   1   2   3   4

2. Disaster Planning

    0   1   2   3   4

3. Disaster Recovery Training

    0   1   2   3   4

4. Care and Handling of Library Materials

    0   1   2   3   4

5. Brittle Book Identification

    0   1   2   3   4

6. Brittle Book Replacement Decisionmaking

    0   1   2   3   4

7. Commercial Binding

    0   1   2   3   4

8. Orientation to Preservation Office Functions

    0   1   2   3   4

9. Orientation to Conservation Services

    0   1   2   3   4

10. Presentation of National Issues/Trends
    0   1   2   3   4
11. Guidelines for Treatment Options: Book Repair, Bindery Prep., Conservation and Preservation
    0   1   2   3   4
12. Preservation exhibits in the Graduate Library
    0   1   2   3   4
13. On-site consultations
    0   1   2   3   4
14. Distribution of preservation handbook fliers
    0   1   2   3   4

Do you have additional comments or questions, or specific workshops to recommend?

_____

_____

_____

Part 2: Supervisory Staff Questionnaire

If you supervise library staff, please complete the following section

1. Please check each job family you supervise: ___ Clerical ___ P & A ___ Librarian ___ Student Assistant
2. Please check all that apply to your position: ___Divisional Library ___ Technical Services ___ Public Services ___ Administrative Services
3. Length of employment in UM Library: ___ less than 1 year ___ 1–4 years ___ 5–10 years ___ more than 10 years
4. Job Family: ___ clerical ___ librarian ___ P & A ___ AFSCME
5. Least desirable time for you to attend training sessions:
   least desirable days of week: ___ Monday ___ Tuesday ___ Wednesday ___ Thursday ___ Friday
   least desirable times of day: ___AM ___PM
   least desirable months: ___ September ___ October ___ November ___ December ___ January ___ February ___ March ___ April ___ May ___ June ___ July ___ August

(Please circle your interest level for each topic)
(No Interest=0   Low=1   Moderate=2   High=3   No Opinion=4)

Motivation

1. How can I get my staff to take a real interest in their jobs?
   0   1   2   3   4
2. What can I do to encourage good work?
   0   1   2   3   4
3. What can I do with the employee who knows how but doesn't do a good job?
   0   1   2   3   4
4. How can I get my staff to do what obviously needs doing without having to be told?
   0   1   2   3   4

Delegation

5. What things should I delegate to my staff and what things must I do myself?

    0   1   2   3   4

6. What can I do about employees who want more responsibility than they can handle?

    0   1   2   3   4

7. What can I do about employees who don't want as much responsibility as they can handle?

    0   1   2   3   4

8. How much leeway should I give my staff in deciding what to do and how to do it?

    0   1   2   3   4

Problem Solving

9. How should I choose the best of several ways of doing a job?

    0   1   2   3   4

10. When faced with a difficult situation, how should I identify the real problem?

    0   1   2   3   4

11. What's the best way to cut a big, complicated problem into pieces I can handle?

    0   1   2   3   4

12. How can I know the best time to make a decision?

    0   1   2   3   4

Hiring/Training

13. How can I tell if my staff members really know how to do their jobs?

    0   1   2   3   4

14. What are some practical, step by step approaches I could use in training my staff?

    0   1   2   3   4

15. How can I tell when training is really needed?

    0   1   2   3   4

16. How should I fill a vacancy on my staff?

    0   1   2   3   4

17. How can I improve my interviewing skills?

    0   1   2   3   4

18. What should be considered when making a selection decision?

    0   1   2   3   4

19. How can I help my staff learn to deal with change?

    0   1   2   3   4

Performance

20. How should I set work standards for my staff?

    0   1   2   3   4

21. How can I evaluate my staff's performance fairly?

    0   1   2   3   4

22. What's the best way to correct poor performance?

    0   1   2   3   4

23. How much should I get involved with personal problems of my staff?

    0   1   2   3   4

Planning

24. What should I consider when planning the work of my group?
    0   1   2   3   4
25. How can I know if the work is going as planned?
    0   1   2   3   4
26. How can I anticipate problems which might block finishing the work?
    0   1   2   3   4
27. How can I stimulate more suggestions from my staff?
    0   1   2   3   4
28. How can I get my staff to cooperate with new ways of doing things?
    0   1   2   3   4
29. How can I sell new ideas to my supervisor?
    0   1   2   3   4
30. How can I sell new ideas to my colleagues?
    0   1   2   3   4

Time Management

31. How can I get my staff to make better use of their time?
    0   1   2   3   4
32. How can I manage demands upon my time by other people?
    0   1   2   3   4
33. How can I make better use of my time each day?
    0   1   2   3   4
34. How can I reduce my demands upon the time of other people?
    0   1   2   3   4

Teamwork

35. How can I get my people to work more effectively as a team?
    0   1   2   3   4
36. What can I do about personality clashes among people on my staff?
    0   1   2   3   4
37. What can I do about people who are not carrying their share of the load?
    0   1   2   3   4
38. How can I get my group to work smoothly with other groups?
    0   1   2   3   4

Communication

39. What does top management really expect of its supervisors?
    0   1   2   3   4
40. How can I give instructions so I get the results I'm after?
    0   1   2   3   4
41. How can I tell if I am communicating effectively with my boss?
    0   1   2   3   4
42. How can I improve the meetings held with my staff?
    0   1   2   3   4

43. How can I handle people's bad suggestions without discouraging future suggestions?

   0   1   2   3   4

Preservation

As of July 30, 1985, seven fliers for the Preservation Handbook have been distributed to Unit Heads. Please place a check mark in the column which most closely describes your staff's reaction to those first seven fliers.

Flier Title:	Useful	Not Useful	Not Seen
1. Brittleness Testing	_____	_____	_____
2. Use of Preservation Supplies	_____	_____	_____
3. Commercial Binding Options	_____	_____	_____
4. Replacement Decisionmaking	_____	_____	_____
5. Food and Drink	_____	_____	_____
6. Environmental #1: Heat and Humidity	_____	_____	_____
7. Environmental #2: Mold and Mildew	_____	_____	_____

Do you have additional comments or questions, or specific workshops to recommend?

10 How to Set Goals

Eva L. Kiewitt

Derive Staff-Development Goals from Institutional Goals

Check your library's **statement of mission**. The goals of your staff-development program should support the mission of the library.

Look over your library's **written standards**. Goals set for your staff-development program should support and not conflict with these standards.

Synchronize your staff-development goals with the library's short- and long-term planning efforts. For example, in two years the on-line catalog will include all bibliographic records, and the card catalog will be removed. Within five years the catalog will contain a number of external databases, and all information will be accessible from remote sites. These planned goals should be reflected in your staff-development program. How do staff need to be prepared for these changes?

Review **unit or departmental goals** to see which ones relate to staff-development needs.

Identify ways your library can assess staff needs and job effectiveness. Incorporate the findings into staff-development goals.

Analyze **technological or managerial changes** within your library. How have these changes affected, or how will they affect, individual jobs? How should they affect your staff-development program?

Ask the Necessary Questions

There are no "right" answers to these questions. The decisions you make will depend upon your organization—upon its size, mission, and mode of operation.

Who should be involved in setting the staff-development goals? Should you include all staff and administration, only the department and unit heads, or outside consultants?

How much time should be spent on goal setting? Are special meetings or retreats needed or can the planning be done within the regularly scheduled meetings?

Who will review the goals and set the priorities? Should the director, a personnel officer, or a committee make the decisions concerning the most pressing needs? Who determines short- or long-range goals?

What other libraries have staff-development goals that would aid in planning? What relevant films, speakers, or workshops are available? Do nonlibrary groups have resources for, or interest in, combining staff-development sessions on issues such as time management?

How can the most **widespread support** for the goals be obtained? Is it necessary to hold special meetings and retreats or to have a planning committee disseminate and explain the goals?

Evaluate Your Staff-Development Goals

Can your goals be translated into **measurable objectives**?

Are the goals **realistic**? Can you afford the time and finances needed to accomplish them? For example, if your goal is to improve computer knowledge, can you provide the in-house training or the needed funds for attendance at workshops or courses?

Can the long-range goals be planned in **stages**?

Are the goals **understandable**? Do they make sense to staff?

How often should staff-development goals be **reevaluated**? Should they be checked quarterly, semiannually, or annually?

Achieving the Goals

Does the staff-development program have special **limitations**? How much can be accomplished without additional funding or released time?

Who will decide if the goals are accomplished or the project needs to be continued? Will the administration or a personnel officer take this responsibility or delegate it to a committee or unit heads?

How will the accomplishment of goals affect staff morale, knowledge, and performance? Are the goals **relevant** enough to increase the skills and effectiveness of staff members? Will reaching the goals give individual staff members greater satisfaction and opportunity for growth?

What are the consequences of reaching or not reaching a goal? Will this affect evaluations of individual or group accomplishment? Will the achievement of some goals be rewarded with special recognition or merit increase?

11 How to Pay for Programs

Lynn C. Badger

How Much Are You Currently Spending on Staff Development?

Even if you do not have a formal program, you are spending money on staff development. The supplies used in creating training manuals, the time spent on training and orienting employees by your supervisors, transportation expenses needed to send a staff member to a workshop in another city all are examples of staff-development costs that you probably are already incurring.

While determining how much money will be needed on both a short-term and a continuing basis, you may find it helpful to estimate roughly how much was spent on staff development in the past. You may be surprised to learn that a considerable amount of money is already being spent. (Good news—with a planned staff-development program you will almost certainly reap much greater benefits for the staff and the library from the dollars spent, even if there is no increase in funding.)

How Do You Determine the Cost of Staff Development?

Estimating the budget for a staff-development program is not easy, especially in the beginning. Keeping **detailed records** of costs over a period of time will greatly facilitate the budget and planning process. One thing to remember: **When starting a new program, the actual total cost is usually greater than originally anticipated.**

Some staff-development costs are obvious, such as the fee paid to an outside trainer who conducts a workshop for your staff. Other costs are sometimes overlooked, such as the salary of a catalog librarian who prepares and presents a training program on searching the on-line catalog. What is most overlooked are any **"opportunity costs"** to the library. For example, books that go uncataloged because the librarian was engaged in staff development activities would be considered an opportunity cost.

As many costs as possible should be estimated, the logical sources for funding the costs should be considered, and ways to trim costs should be identified. The following lists identify common staff-development program costs.

Visible Costs
Fees for outside speakers
Transportation, lodging, and meals for outside speakers
Room rental or auditorium fee
Rental or purchase price of training materials and equipment
Registration fees and transportation for participants
Production costs for slides or transparencies
Duplication costs
Refreshments

Hidden Costs
Administrative overhead
Salary of staff members who function as trainers
Salary of staff members attending programs
Cost of planning and evaluation
Opportunity costs (what does not get done while staff-development activities are conducted)

Where Can Funding Be Obtained for a Staff-Development Program?

Funding for staff development normally comes from the **operating-expenses** (as opposed to the materials) budget of the library.

Since competition for funds is usually keen, you must be able to show that the program is based on carefully assessed needs and on clearly developed objectives. The need for funds should be viewed on both a short-term (program-start-up) and long-range (program-maintenance) basis.

To sustain the program, the library administration will expect a **careful accounting** of where the money goes and of what benefits have been derived.

While the major source of staff-development funds is the library budget, consider **seeking supplemental funds** from the sources listed below. Brainstorming may produce additional funding sources unique to your location or organization.

Consider the following:

Parent organization (municipality, university, library system, or corporation)

Friends of the Library groups

Library-staff associations

Other libraries, library associations, and library schools (for sponsored programs or exchange programs for individuals)

Programs, internships, and fellowships for library staff (for example: Council of Library Resources [CLR] internships)

Grants from state, regional, or federal sources (for example: H. W. Wilson Library Staff Development Grant, a cash grant of $2,500 administered by the ALA Awards Committee)

How Can My Library Stretch Its Staff-Development Dollar?

No library ever seems to have as much to spend for staff development as is needed. The following tips will help you get the most from your staff-development dollar.

Low Cost Staff-Development Activities

Many staff-development activities demand little in the way of out-of-pocket expense. Such activities should be affordable during even the leanest years.

Lunch talks (brown-bag lunches featuring a staff member talking about a conference attended, an article or book, or an interest)

Library newsletter

In-house staff-exchange program

Journal club (staff with common interests meet to discuss recent research)

Mentor program

Orientation programs for new employees

Resource Sharing

Sharing resources almost always results in lowered costs. Keep in mind the potential disadvantages of resource sharing: a program designed for another library may be unsuited to your library and may attract attendees with differing backgrounds and goals. In some cases, the disadvantages can outweigh the savings.

Establish **reciprocal arrangements** with local or regional libraries to send your staff to their programs in exchange for their staff attending yours.

Send speakers from your library to another library in exchange for their experts assisting with your programs.

Volunteer to host a workshop at which staff from other libraries from the area will be invited. (In many cases the host institution is given a registration-fee discount.)

Consider adapting staff-development materials from other libraries for use in your program. (The LAMA PAS Staff Development Committee maintains a staff-development programs and policies clearinghouse).

Making Wise Choices

It is important to know when to choose an outside versus an inside expert or when to bring in a speaker or to send your staff to an outside workshop. Many factors should be considered when making these decisions. (*See* chapter 12 on how to find expert speakers or presenters.) Keep in mind the following factors:

Using a staff member as a speaker-trainer is almost always cheaper than paying an outside expert, but do not forget the hidden costs. It may be more economical to develop a group of in-house trainers.

Compare the costs of hiring a trainer with the benefits to the participants. Generally speaking, the more staff members that need training, the easier it is to justify paying an outside expert to come to your library.

If only a few employees need training, consider sending them to an outside workshop.

Miscellaneous Cost-cutting Tips

Take advantage of the speakers, training manuals, and audio-visual aids available from the personnel or administrative office of the parent (municipal, university, or corporate) institution.

When choosing an outside expert, consider volunteers with appropriate expertise (library associations sometimes maintain lists).

Consider local experts from universities, colleges, community adult-education organizations, or government agencies. Their fees, if any, may be smaller than those of nonlocal experts. You will also save travel and lodging expenses.

Send staff members to training classes offered by community adult-education or civil-service programs; this may prove less costly than developing your own program.

Train someone on your staff to be a trainer (see chapter 18).

Regularly evaluate each of your staff-development activities; eliminate any that are not worthwhile.

Plan staff-development activities to achieve more than a single purpose.

12 How to Find Expert Speakers or Presenters

Lynn C. Badger

Should the Expert Come from Inside or Outside the Library?

Many factors come into play when making the decision of whether to use an expert (consultant, speaker, presenter, or trainer) from inside or outside the library. The following checklist outlines key questions to be asked before the decision is made; the summary table lists the advantages of choosing either alternate.

Checklist of Considerations

1. Are there staff members with the knowledge, training skills, and the willingness to conduct the program? Have you considered the advantages, in addition to the lower costs, of using your own staff—e.g., the creation of a sense of **self-sufficiency** in the library and the increased knowledge and efficiency gained by staff resource persons through training others?
2. Will your **staff-development budget** allow you to pay an outside speaker's fee or the travel and registration costs for staff members to attend workshops outside the library?
3. Have you considered the **hidden costs** of using your own staff, such as lost time associated with regular job responsibilities?
4. Does the presenter need to have in-depth knowledge of a situation (procedures, equipment, etc.) unique to your library? If so, an external resource person may be inappropriate.
5. How many staff members will be participating in the program? Paying an outside expert's fee may be more justifiable if a large number of staff will be involved. If the number is small, and using a staff member as a presenter is unfeasible, consider sending the participants to the workshop, rather than bringing the workshop to the library.

61

6. How essential to the success of the program are the **fresh ideas**, new approaches, and different viewpoints that an external speaker may introduce? Do participants need to interact with new people and to experience a different environment? If yes, consider sending staff to an outside workshop or opening an in-house program to staff from other libraries.

7. Do you expect extensive **preplanning or follow-up** training to be necessary? How will this be handled if an outside expert is chosen?

8. How important to the success of the program is the presence of a well-known expert? Does the workshop call for the appearance of **neutrality and objectivity**, which may be associated with an outside resource person?

Summary of Possible Advantages:

Staff-Member Expert
Available at lower cost (no fees, travel expenses, etc.)
Creates a sense of self-sufficiency among library staff
Has in-depth knowledge of the library and its policies
Enhances team spirit
Gains increased knowledge through training others
Is easily accessible for needed follow-up

Outside Expert
Brings in fresh ideas, new approaches, and different viewpoints
May lend the appearance of neutrality and objectivity
Is needed in sensitive situations
May be more experienced at teaching and evaluation
May have greater credibility and authority

What to Consider When Locating a Resource Person on Your Staff

1. Some in-house resource persons may be easily identifiable: they are already serving as the trainers or the experts for their departments or for the entire library. But there may be others on the staff with the expertise, ability, and interest in training who have yet to be identified. A survey of the staff could bring these resources and talents to light.

2. Remember that an interest in training and the possession of technical or subject knowledge are not enough: your inside expert must also have the **ability to train** in order to be effective. Although you may be saving money, you may not be truly profiting by using staff members who know their fields but who lack the ability or skills to teach others.

3. Your library may wish to bring in an outside expert to train a group of staff members in training techniques. Training consultant firms provide this type of training (usually referred to as facilitator training).

How to Find a Resource Person Outside Your Library

Library-related Contacts

1. Take advantage of other libraries in the area that have identified speakers and presenters. Discuss the possibility of a reciprocal agreement whereby you send your staff to their programs in exchange for their staff attending yours. Another consideration: jointly sponsor a workshop.
2. Contact library colleagues for the names of experts whom they have used or seen used successfully in similar situations. Get advice on other persons and places to turn to for leads.
3. Contact library-school faculty.
4. Contact state or regional library agencies.
5. Printed programs from past library association conferences include the names of speakers and leaders at conferences and preconference workshops.
6. Library associations often keep lists of speakers or consultants, clearinghouses, and workshops. Examples:

   The ALA Office for Library Personnel Resources (OLPR) publishes a list of the ALA divisions that maintain speakers' bureaus.

   The Library Administration and Management Association (LAMA) publishes a list of library consultants.

   The LAMA PAS Staff Development Committee maintains a staff-development programs and policies clearinghouse.

   The Association of College and Research Libraries (ACRL) sponsors regional continuing-education programs.

   The Association of Research Libraries (ARL) Office of Management Studies hosts institutes on a number of different library staff-development topics.

Contacts within the Organization-at-Large

1. Take advantage of organization-wide personnel or training offices: i.e., those within your municipal government or university.
2. Contact your parent organization's administrative offices for the names of persons within the organization who possess expertise in a given area.
3. Contact educational institutions for the names of faculty and training personnel at local community colleges, colleges, and universities.
4. Contact community adult-education organizations and the local school board.
5. The American Association for Adult and Continuing Education (202-822-7866) and the American Society for Training and Development (703-683-8100) have local and regional chapters throughout the nation that may be called for suggestions about speakers and training programs.

Business and Industry

1. Personnel offices of local businesses often have lists of experts that they have used for employee training and development.
2. Contact local business associations and local government and civic organizations.
3. Check your own library's collection for directories of consultants.

Authors

1. Contact the author of a book or article on the topic of your program to discuss the possibility of his or her serving as your expert.
2. If the author you want is unavailable, ask him or her to provide you with the names of other qualified experts.

13 How to Prepare for a Specific Program

Anne Grodzins Lipow

The preparations stage, as defined here, assumes that you have already decided to present a particular program and that the reasons for doing so are clear.

Basic Rules

1. **Allow sufficient time.** Preparations take more time than you think. Four months is usually the minimum for most programs that involve presenters, publicity, handouts, and enrollment; six months are required for programs that rely on a number of people and involve a multiplicity of arrangements.
2. **Check out the speaker(s) and instructor(s).** If you are unfamiliar with them, confirm their effectiveness by asking others with first-hand experience. Talk to previous client(s); ask to see *all* the evaluations of one or two recent sessions.
3. **Draft a "to-do" list**—triple-spaced to leave room for explanatory notes. Be specific.
   Poor: "Contact speaker." "Make room arrangements."
   Better: "Contact speaker (555-1001) about topic, title of topic, coverage, description/level of audience, expected degree of learning, length of session, length of time speaker needs to set up room, equipment requirements, arrangement of room, fee and when to expect payment, and follow-up recommendations . . . " "Make room arrangements: size, flexibility of seating, outlets for electrical equipment, ventilation, proximity to eating/bathroom facilities . . . "
4. **Establish a timetable of tentative deadlines** and mark them on your calendar.

5. **Expect things to go wrong.** When you think that you have the planning under control, ask yourself, "What can go wrong?" and take preventative or backup measures. Repeat these steps about a week before the event.

6. **Include follow-up plans in your preparations.** Prevent "transfer failure" (failure of participant to use the new skills on the job). Do not wait until after the program to plan follow-up sessions.

Checklist of Preparation Steps

Early Preparations

1. **Contact speaker(s).** Agree on the dates, length of session(s), speaker's requirements for room arrangements and equipment, fee (if any), expenses (meals, lodging, transportation), production of speaker's handouts, and maximum and minimum attendance.

2. **Reach a general agreement with each speaker about matters important to *you*.** Discuss the library's objectives, target audience, desirable format (whether to use lectures, participation, practice time, role playing, or bibliography), and ideas for follow up.

3. Send the speaker **a memorandum confirming your understanding of the agreement**. Include a list of all available equipment (e.g., transparency projector, screen, blackboard, chalk, easel pad, flow pens, masking tape, computer support [software, terminal settings, modem, phone]). Check off those requested by the speaker. Include your estimate of attendance. Provide a rough drawing of the room arrangement as the speaker requested it (e.g., long tables arranged in a U-shape; small scattered tables seating four each). **Request return confirmation** within two weeks.

4. **Establish tentative target dates** or deadlines for each activity or portion of an activity, and notify those on whom you are relying of the relevant dates. For example:

   Speaker(s): Due dates for a brief description of the session for publicity purposes; master copy of bibliography and other handouts; speaker's confirmation of room arrangements and equipment needs.

   Secretary: When to expect draft copy of printed material; when final copy is due. When to expect master copy, if you are only printing. Dates for sending out publicity, enrollment forms, confirmation of enrollment, and reminder of enrollment. Dates should be related to the anticipated amount of material to be produced.

   Technician (backup in case of equipment failure): Date for practice session, date of program.

   Enrollees: Due date for submitting enrollment form; deadline to submit postsession report/assignment.

   Graphic artist: When to meet to discuss design for publicity; deadline for camera-ready copy.

   Supervisors: Deadlines for confirming their agreement with program, their expectations of the outcome, and their commitment to providing a postsession learning environment.

5. **Draft publicity campaign and produce the products.**

Posters/fliers: Distribute to what addresses?
Articles: For what publications?
Mailings: To what groups?
Verbal announcements: At what meetings? Who should announce?
Have at least two people proofread carefully.

Timetable

4–6 Weeks before Program

Distribute publicity, announcements, enrollment forms.

2–4 Weeks before Program

Meet with or contact speaker(s) to review final details.
Order refreshments.
Prepare evaluation form for enrollees to submit at end of session (include address for mailing if submitting later). Prepare follow-up evaluation form to mail to enrollees two weeks after session.
Prepare packets for enrollees. Make extra copies for interested nonparticipants to distribute after the program. Include evaluation form.
Send confirmation to enrollees. Include building and room number, map, special instructions (parking).
Pencils and pads for attendees?
Arrange for assistance with room setup and "gofer" chores on the day of program.
Confirm whereabouts/availability/working condition of audiovisual/computer equipment.
Inform speaker(s) of who will be attending.

Preprogram Steps

Prepare name tags (write first name in large letters with thick-point pen).
Prepare list of attendees to include in packet.
Arrange for brief (three-to-five-minute) welcome presentation by the library director, another administrator, or an appropriate spokesperson.
Review all arrangements. Remind assistants—refreshments provider, standby technician—of upcoming dates and deadlines.

D-Day

Set up equipment.
Arrange seating in room.
Keep tally of attendees, no-shows.

Postprogram Steps

Tabulate attendance.

Summarize evaluations.

Hold postmortem with speaker(s).

Implement all follow-up activities that were planned, to provide continued-learning support required for successful transfer of training—post-session assignment, coaching agreements, practice time, check-up phone calls.

Meet with attendees' supervisors/department heads to find out how session affected performance and whether desired outcomes were attained.

Write report of program and circulate it to all appropriate people.

Tips to Prevent Common Problems

Potential Problem	Tip
You have no idea who or how many will attend.	Require enrollment. On enrollment form, solicit information about interests; level of knowledge; background of experience, training.
Audience is too advanced for session or too inexperienced.	Publicity should clearly state intended audience and what will be covered.
Participants forgot to attend session.	Send reminder just before session.
Meeting place is hard to find.	Send map to participants.
Room is badly arranged.	Provide drawing of how you want seating. Arrive ahead of time to rearrange.
Speaker's timing is off.	Clarify time limits for each speaker. Appoint a timekeeper who signals when 5, 1, and 0 minutes are left.
Speaker's voice is too soft.	Provide microphone. Appoint someone at back of room to signal speaker to talk louder.
Spelling or factual errors appear in handouts.	Ask at least one other person to proofread.
Computer equipment fails.	Test equipment first; prepare handouts as adequate substitute.

14 How to Improve Visual Aids

Anne Grodzins Lipow

Visual aids can make the difference between a good presentation and an excellent one. Any oral presentation can be improved by graphic support—by brief lists or simple drawings projected onto a screen at the front of the room or by coordinated handouts distributed to the audience. Visuals can say in a picture (or list) what it would take paragraphs to say in words. And, if done well, the message they convey will be remembered longer than the same message delivered by spoken words alone. Visual aids are especially important for the members of your audience who learn best by *seeing* new ideas and information as opposed to *hearing* them. Visual aids not only help your audience to follow and understand your presentation; they also help to keep you on track.

To make effective visual aids, you do not need to be an artist or a calligrapher. Merely select the right medium for your presentation, follow some simple guidelines, and you will be surprised at the benefits to both you and your audience.

Types of Visual Aids

Transparency Overheads

Advantages

Transparencies can be produced quickly and are easily portable. They can be made from copying book pages, photographs, or original works, or they can be created on the spot, using special marking pencils. They can be displayed in black-and-white or color and can be shown in a lighted room, which helps stimulate discussion and enables the audience to take notes. Transparencies can be manipulated, modified, and built upon during your presentation and are appropriate for small or large audiences.

Disadvantages

Some speakers find them difficult to change and handle. They must be stored with care to prevent wrinkles.

Easel Paper and Flipcharts

Advantages

Easel paper and flipcharts add a personal touch to your presentation. They give you a large area in which to work and can be changed and expanded during your presentation. Easy to handle and to read in a lighted room, they tend to stimulate discussion (so allow extra time for comments).

Disadvantages

They are less portable and durable than transparencies. The presenter may need to practice flipping the pages. Flipcharts are inappropriate for very large audiences.

Cautions and Tips

Use a 27-by-34-inch pad, preferably with lined paper or with lines lightly penciled onto the surface.

Make large, bold letters and illustrations. Use broad-tipped markers. Select water-soluble markers, not indelible-ink, which will soak through to the next page. Choose high-contrast colored markers (e.g., black-on-white); avoid light colors, particularly yellow. Sketch your text in light pencil first to ensure good spacing and correct spelling.

Leave the first two pages of the pad blank to prevent the audience from reading in advance. Or, on the first page, display a graphic relevant to your talk, special instructions to the audience, the title of your talk, or other visual.

Leave a blank page or two between every written page so the next page does not show through. Staple the left and right corners of the pages together to make turning easier.

If you create the page as you are making the presentation, remember to write large.

If you will be paging back and forth during your presentation, place labeled tabs (which you can make out of masking tape) along the underside, for ease of flipping.

Tearing sheets off the pad and taping them to the wall allows you and the audience to refer easily back to material already covered. But the tear-tape-hang sequence can be awkward and waste time. Here are some tips to make that process go smoothly.

Before the session starts, stick several precut pieces of tape along the leg of the easel, ready for use.

Before you tear off a sheet, place two pieces of tape at the top of the sheet—each a couple of inches from the left and right edges—so that half of each piece is sticking to the sheet and half extends above it.

With your fingers at the perforation, start about an inch of tear along the top right of the sheet.

Then grab the lower right corner of the sheet and pull down diagonally to the left. The tape at the top will remain with the torn-off sheet.

The result will be a ready-to-mount sheet.

If you plan only a one-page display, consider using butcher paper, available at art-supply stores. It is less expensive than easel paper and is made of sturdier stock so the ink does not soak through. You can roll it up (keeping the writing on the *outside*), store it, and re-use it.

35mm Slides

Advantages

Slides are portable; one slide tray holds up to eighty slides. They are light and convenient for carrying in a briefcase. Slides provide a polished look and can achieve special effects. They are appropriate for auditoriums, large conference rooms, and groups of fifty or more.

Disadvantages

Slides are more expensive than other formats and require more time and expertise to produce. They must be shown in a darkened room, which discourages discussion and note taking.

Computer Presentation Software

Advantages

Screens are easy to develop, professional, and easy to update. They can display moving images and allow for the integration of graphic, textual, and sound representations.

Disadvantages

They require special (sometimes expensive) hardware and software and considerable practice before they can be used.

Handout Materials

Do's and Don'ts

Provide space on each page for note taking.

Distribute handouts before the session begins. Do not distract the audience by passing them out during your presentation. Do not wait until the end of the session to distribute handouts. The audience will take more efficient notes prompted by your handouts than they could by creating them from scratch and will, therefore, be able to pay better attention to your oral presentation.

(Note taking is an important way for the audience to internalize and remember what you are presenting. Facilitating note-taking maximizes the audience's chances of learning.)

Make certain that you have enough handouts for the entire audience.

Review the contents with your audience at the outset to be sure each person has the full set.

Package the handouts so that the audience is not constantly shuffling paper.

Place all sheets in a binder or folder.

Place sheets in the order in which you will refer to them.

Paginate and label sections and subsections, for easy referral.

Include an attractive title-and-contents page with the date and your name and affiliation.

Include copies of *all* informational overheads in your handouts.

Common Mistakes and How to Prevent Them

Mistake   Visual does not relate to the speaker's point

Antidote   Make your visual reinforce your objective(s).
Give your visual a label that relates to the text of the oral presentation.

Mistake   Too much information

Antidote   Fold a piece of 8-1/2-by-11-inch paper into quarters and print your text on one of the quarters. If you cannot read the text from an arm's length away, you have too much information for one visual.

Beware of crowding too many points onto one visual; instead, divide the material into separate visuals or give the audience a copy of the visual so that they use the overhead for reference only. Visuals should support spoken words, not replace them.

Mistake   List contains too many points

Antidote   Each list should contain no more than from three to five points. If your list is longer, reorganize it into smaller clusters around subheadings.

Mistake   Visual duplicates oral presentation

Antidote   Paraphrase; do not read the visual as it appears. It should speak for itself or make the point in a different way. It should always enhance your presentation. The best visuals are those that *briefly* emphasize your key points. Uncomplicated photographs, illustrations, and colored charts and graphs can help the audience understand your message. Flowcharts, data tables, and organizational charts often are too detailed.

Mistake   Illegible words

Antidote   Make your words big and bold. Use only about 12 words per visual.

Mistake   Too many visuals

Antidote   Presentations often use more visuals than necessary. The appropriate number depends on the specific presentation. For example, a highly technical talk might require spending several minutes on each of a few visuals. A general talk might call for one visual per each major point in your outline.

Mistake   Monotonous visuals

Antidote   Vary the content and character of the visuals. Use combinations of lists, drawings, and charts.

Questions Relevant to Visual Formats

1. Who is my audience?
2. How many people will be in the audience? How large is the room? How large should the visuals be?
3. How much time will it take to prepare the visuals?
4. Are the equipment and materials available? Is there money to pay for them?
5. How many times will I be giving this presentation? If more than once, can the visuals be used, or easily adapted, for a variety of audiences?

Color Considerations

1. Consider the background color when planning your visual.

   Most legible: High-contrast colors such as black on white or yellow; strong green or blue on white.
   Least legible: Red on green.

2. Use color with restraint. Err on the side of fewer colors. Get a second opinion.

Choosing the Right Graphic Representations

To Show:	Use:
A group of related items in no specific order	A bulleted list
	A numbered list if the total number is important
	A list in which each item is preceded by a picture, icon, or graphic to aid in comprehension and enhance recollection
A group of related items in a specific order	A numbered list
Relationships and steps involved in a process	Flowchart or process diagram
An evaluation of items against several criteria	Rating table
A comparison of several things in relation to one variable	Bar graph or pie chart
A concept	Simple illustration

15 How to Make Training Stick

Deborah A. Carver

Transfer of training can be enhanced by a few simple procedures performed by the trainer, the participant, and the participant's supervisor. It is important to remember that training will not result automatically in increased ability levels unless some of these additional steps are taken. Depending upon the organization, some steps may be more effective than others.

What the Trainer Can Do

The trainer can take the lead in ensuring transfer. Although the participant and the manager share this responsibility, the trainer is in the best position to encourage transfer strategies.

1. **Find out as much as possible about the library** or the unit within the library where the training will occur. This advice holds as true for trainers who are part of the organization as it does for those who are hired from the outside. Know what people do, how they are rewarded, and what the goals are.
2. **Identify any likely barriers.** If resistance is strong, training may fail to produce the desired results.
3. **Solicit the interest and support of managers** early in the process. Familiarize managers with the concepts and principles of the training program but avoid forcing disinterested managers into playing a more active role.
4. Distribute a set of **advance reading materials** or assignments to participants. State the training objectives and specify what participants will be expected to do differently following the training session.

5. **Test the knowledge** of participants beforehand. This process will enlighten the audience as to how much they do not know, which can increase their interest in the program.
6. **Train intact groups** rather than selecting one individual from each unit. Peer-group support is a major factor in determining whether newly learned skills will transfer.
7. Focus on **a few related concepts**. Do not go overboard trying to jam too many points into a single session. Depth is more important than breadth.
8. Provide trainees with as much detailed and **individualized instruction** on how and when to use the new skills as possible. (This requires a certain degree of job knowledge on the part of the trainer.)
9. Allow participants to **practice** the skills during the training session. If time permits, allow practice beyond the point at which a procedure or skill can be done correctly. One successful attempt is often insufficient to guarantee transfer.
10. Discuss the **concept of transfer** with the participants.
11. At the end of the session, give the participants **appropriate job aids,** such as checklists or reference manuals.
12. Arrange for **follow-up contacts** to provide support and respond to difficulties encountered in the application of the skills. Consider offering a refresher course that deals with the problems of implementation.
13. If the resources are available, consider **posttraining evaluation** to measure performance improvements.

What the Trainee Can Do

Employees need to take an active role in their own professional development. When something is missing from the training program, such as a follow-up session, ask if it may be included.

1. When possible, select training programs to **meet existing interests and job needs.** If a staff-development needs analysis has not been done, participants should suggest specific programs which they think will be useful.
2. **Prepare** as much as possible before the training session. If materials have not been distributed, ask the trainer to suggest one or two articles which discuss the concepts to be covered in the program.
3. Constantly think of possible **on-the-job applications** throughout the workshop.
4. **Document efforts** made between the training program and any follow-up session to use the new skills. Note any difficulties, and plan to share these with the trainer.
5. Refer frequently to course materials, action plans, and training contracts.

6. Form **support groups** with others who have attended the training session. Discuss strategies and obstacles related to implementation.

What the Manager Can Do

Perhaps the most overlooked aspect of the training process has been the role of the manager or supervisor. If an employee's supervisor is interested in the training program, expects to see results, and intends to recognize and reward the use of new skills and knowledge on the job, then the chances of transfer are greatly increased.

1. **Avoid packaged programs** that are too general. Participants have greater difficulty relating to situations that have little to do with their own work.
2. Consider **abandoning existing programs** which have not resulted in measurable improvement. Ineffective training is not only wasteful, it can be detrimental.
3. Select several **employees from a single library unit.** This will increase the likelihood that concepts taught in the training session will be discussed back on the job.
4. Initially, send employees who are **involved in their jobs** and interested in improving their performance. While these individuals may not need the training as much as others, their enthusiasm may help build interest among other employees.
5. **Meet with the trainer** beforehand to discuss existing problems, relevant examples, and appropriate follow-up strategies. Select a project whch will enable employees to use the new skills once they return to work.
6. **Preview instructional materials** for accuracy and relevance.
7. Become familiar with the skills and terminology which will be covered in the program.
8. Notify employees well in advance of the program. **Encourage preparation**.
9. **Meet with participants** before the training begins. Go over the objectives and indicate support for the program.
10. Release trainees from normal duties and distractions during the training period. If possible, arrange for the training to take place **outside the library**.
11. Meet with participants immediately following the training session. Discuss possible on-the-job applications. **Reinforce any effort to use new skills.**
12. Arrange for trainees to **share their experience** with other employees. Make sure that trainees know that they will be expected to do this before they participate in the program.
13. Provide **low-risk opportunities** for participants to try out their new skills on the job.
14. Arrange for **subsequent training** to build on skills already learned.

Most of these suggestions require little cost but have great benefit. Think of previous training programs that have taken place in your library. Chances are that most of them could have been improved by adding one or more of these steps. Understanding the concept of transfer and the conditions that impede or promote it will help make training and staff-development programs worthwhile. When you ensure some level of transfer, your training dollars will go farther.

16 How to Make an Effective Presentation

Anne Grodzins Lipow

Every effective presentation has three components: sufficient preparation, competent delivery, and supportive visual aids. Chapter 14 provides guidelines for producing visual aids that can strengthen your presentation. This chapter highlights the ingredients that make up the other two components.

Sufficient Preparation

Never underestimate the importance of preparation. "It takes three weeks," Mark Twain once said, "to prepare a good ad-lib speech." Here are the five primary steps of the preparation process:

1. Complete this sentence: "After attending my presentation, my audience will know/know how to/be able to . . . . "
2. **Define your audience** and its need. Who needs to know this information? Why? What prior knowledge is required?
3. Organize your talk around no more than **three to four major points**.
4. **Write a draft**. Then **rewrite** it. Then **speak** it.
   To make an effective presentation, knowing your topic is not enough. There is often a big gap between what you *mean to say* and what you *say*. You need to be able to explain what you know so others can understand. Do not rely solely on an outline—it increases the risk of illogical exposition, hazy description of complex ideas, and sloppy digression. Writing your talk does not mean that you must read what you wrote, but it does provide you with a mirror of your articulated thoughts. To prevent half-formed concepts and mistimed explanations, *write out the speech*.

5. Plan a **lively opening** and a **forceful closing**.

   When you have completed the five steps, answer this question: "Will my audience know what I hoped they would in Step 1?"

Competent Delivery

More important than the words you choose to say is *how* you say them. Eloquent prose can go unheard, and mediocre prose can be inspiring and eagerly heard depending on the delivery. Competent delivery entails a performance; many of the skills required for a competent delivery are those of the performer. Practicing your delivery is the key to a fine presentation, just as rehearsals are the key to a flawless performance. Below is a checklist of the major elements of successful delivery. Check those that you need to pay special attention to, and keep them in mind as you rehearse your presentation. To compensate for any negative delivery habits or characteristics you may have, mark your speech at appropriate places with "stage directions" to remind yourself to take corrective action. For example, do your presentations lack eye contact? Build into your speech places to pan to the audience: look left, center, and right. Do you tend to speak in monotones? Mark your notes with arrows that tell you to say particular words in a raised or lowered tone or to speed up or slow down particular phrases to vary the pace.

Checklist

1. Appearance
   ___ Wear businesslike (undistracting), comfortable clothes.
   ___ Maintain a stable stance.
   ___ Avoid fidgeting (jangling change in the pocket; clicking a ballpoint pen).
2. Voice
   ___ Vary the pitch, but keep it in lower range.
   ___ Check for loudness (most people need to talk louder than usual).
   ___ Check for speed (most people need to talk slower than usual).
   ___ Enunciate clearly; exaggerate words that you tend to slur.
   ___ Inject enthusiasm into your tone.
3. Choice of words
   ___ Use action verbs, and image-conjuring adjectives and nouns.
   ___ Eliminate or define jargon.
4. Pace
   ___ Start aggressively, challengingly.
   ___ Pause or vary loudness and speed for emphasis.
   ___ Vary the length of sentences in a paragraph.
   ___ Intersperse visuals, discussion, and hands-on demonstration throughout the lecture.
   ___ Interject personal asides and anecdotes.

5. Rapport with the audience
   ___ Make good eye contact.
   ___ Build in participatory activity.
   ___ Encourage (leave time for) discussion.
   ___ Know when to cut off discussion.
   ___ Practice supportive (versus argumentative) responses to skeptical questions.

17 How to Evaluate Your Program

Kitty Smith

Why Is Evaluation Important?

Evaluation is the process planners use to find out whether a program or activity is meeting stated objectives and if modifications are necessary to ensure that the desired outcomes are obtained. Evaluation provides information about the current situation and about the degree of success achieved thus far. This kind of information is vital to continued success because it forms the basis for further planning and timely decision making. In other words, evaluation works hand-in-hand with planning to ensure a continuous flow of the knowledge required for assessment, further action, and accountability.

How Can Evaluation Help the Staff-Development Program?

The integration of evaluation into staff-development programs and activities can:

Provide **factual information** for better decisions, accurate recording of accomplishments, and further planning

Ascertain the relative **costs** and **benefits** of a program

Reinforce learning and personal growth

Assess the extent to which **objectives** are being accomplished

Determine which factors have an impact on staff development

Assure **quality control**

Document learning experiences

Defend the institution's investment in staff development and **justify** projected programs

How Can We Get the Most Out of Evaluation?

A Checklist of Questions to Ask Yourself

—How much **importance** do we place on the evaluation process? Is it an integral part of the staff-development program, or merely something that we will "get around to if time permits?"

—Do we understand the **purpose** and importance of evaluation? Do we know what we need to evaluate?

—To what extent does our evaluation process lead to **long-term planning** for staff development? Does our program consist of a series of unrelated "events," with little opportunity for implementing suggested improvements? If so, is there really a need to evaluate? On the other hand, will evaluation have a real impact on our staff-development program planning? Will there be an opportunity to use the information gathered in evaluation to improve what we have done and to plan for the future? If so, do we know what we will do with the information in the short-term and in the long-term?

—What assurances do we have that our evaluation process will yield candid information? Are we committed to **openness** and honesty in the evaluation process?

—Are we prepared to respond to **negative evaluations**? Are we ready to implement suggested improvements in content, format, or style? Are we prepared to meet expressed needs for further staff-development activities or topics? Will participants' suggestions be given serious consideration? Will evaluation information be reflected in the planning and presentation of future staff-development activities?

—Do we know how to conduct a valid and useful evaluation? Do we know how, where, and when to get the data we need for subsequent planning? Is the process **feasible**? Are we willing to spend the time and effort needed to prepare?

—Have we identified the **results we expect** from the program and activities? Do we know what impact we want the program to have on individuals as well as on the organization? Do we expect changed behavior as a result of the activity? If so, how, when, and how often will we check up on it?

—Can we determine which conditions contribute to or impede the success of the program in achieving its objectives?

—Can we find out what kinds of staff-development activities are most successful from the **participants' point of view**? Which topics are the most relevant to job responsibilities? Which methods are most effective and worthwhile?

—Is our purpose for evaluation clear? Are we evaluating the impact of the program on the organization? On employees' job performances? Are we evaluating the effectiveness of specific activities or techniques within the program itself? Have we stated the expected results in terms of our chosen goals and objectives?

—In light of our objectives, who will provide the needed information?

Employees? Supervisors? Management? Instructors? Will their **privacy** be protected? Will the process assess these groups' perceptions of new learning or increased competence? What are the potential rewards for learning?

—Do the evaluations indicate the necessity for a **follow-up** session on the same topics?

—Does the evaluation process measure content **coverage and relevancy**? Activity design? Use of resources? What are the results in relation to expectations, needs, and costs?

—Which evaluation techniques will be used? Performance tests? Questionnaires? Interviews? Observation?

—How will results be analyzed? Reported? Disseminated? Used?

What Kinds of Evaluation Information Should Be Collected?

Some Practical Tips

Keep in mind that your evaluation process must meet the needs of your particular organization.

There are costs involved in evaluating a staff-development program—time, money, materials—and these must be weighed against the anticipated benefits. The cost, however, should never be used as an excuse to avoid evaluation altogether.

Evaluation should not be an afterthought, a last-minute ritual performed by giving participants a makeshift reaction form.

Types of Information to Collect

Demographic information on the participants (e.g., age, sex, type of job, duties)

The current state of participants' knowledge, ability, and attitudes. These could be measured at the beginning and end of a particular activity to assess growth and progress

The participants' expectations at the beginning of the program and their perceptions of how well those expectations were met

The participants' plans to apply what they have learned to their own job or life situations

The participants' perceptions of the content of the activity and the methods used (Was the topic adequately covered? Was it relevant to their needs? Were there areas which were particularly strong or weak?)

Did the results justify the time and expense? Were the objectives accomplished?

What about the Evaluation Questionnaire?

Evaluators may use a variety of methods to collect information from participants, including tests, interviews, observations, and questionnaires. The method you choose depends on a number of factors. The evaluation questionnaire is the method most people are familiar with, and the one that they are most likely to use. Reasons for selecting this method range from lack of expertise in testing to lack of time for in-depth interviews or follow-up observations. The less familiar methods, however, can produce a wealth of useful information if the evaluator can spend a little extra time learning how to apply them.

The questionnaire itself can be made more useful if the evaluator keeps these few ideas in mind:

Ask thoughtful questions, designed to get the information you are seeking. Do not just ask "yes or no" questions.

Do not ask the participants "how they felt" about the activity. You want to measure the effectiveness of the program, not the participants' current emotional state.

Do not use a questionnaire only at the end of the activity. Try using shorter questionnaires interspersed throughout the program to measure the participants' grasp of the content or to reinforce what they have just learned.

Test your questionnaires before using them to be sure that they are interpreted the way you want them to be interpreted.

Administer follow-up questionnaires to the participants at a later date to reinforce their learning and to find out if they have been able to transfer their learning experience to their own job or life situations.

18 How to Develop Training Skills

Wendy L. Scott

Benefits of Developing Training Skills

Many librarians who are expected to perform training and staff-development functions have little or no formal instruction in teaching methods. Some librarians may have received, in the course of their professional education, an introduction to adult-learning concepts, and some institutions have developed conferences, workshops, and manuals on training adult learners. This type of preparation, however, is not widespread.

In addition to increasing the number of people on the staff able to conduct formal staff-development activities, developing the training skills of librarians has a number of benefits. For example, staff with public-service responsibilities can apply the principles of adult education to general-reference services and bibliographic instruction. Another important benefit is improved communication skills.

Selecting Trainers

1. Identify potential trainers through **a survey, referral, or interview**.
2. While expertise is important when selecting someone to do training, it is not the only criterion. Characteristics of good trainers include:

   Concern for learners
   Ability to relate theory to practice
   Self-confidence
   Openness to different approaches
   Ability to listen

> Ability to instill confidence in learners
> Ability to avoid demeaning or punitive action
> Ability to establish a supportive climate

3. Select employees who feel **comfortable "on stage"** and enjoy making presentations. (One organization has had success in selecting trainers with drama backgrounds.)

Methods of Developing Training Skills

1. Bring in an **outside expert** to train staff, or conduct a workshop in-house if you have someone on staff who knows how to instruct trainers.

2. If your library already has one individual, such as a personnel librarian, who is responsible primarily for coordinating training, send him or her to a **conference or institute for special instruction in training skills.**

3. Take full advantage of the **numerous seminars** available on training, facilitation, and presentation skills. The Training Skills Institute sponsored by the Association of Research Library's Office of Management Studies is one such program geared specifically toward libraries.

4. **Written manuals and videos** on planning and conducting workshops, improving on-the-job training skills, speaking effectively, and a wide variety of other training-related topics are available. These materials can help new trainers develop their teaching and planning skills.

5. **Videotaping practice presentations** can be an effective training method. When participants see their own performances, they are less likely to reject criticism and more likely to make appropriate improvements. Group critiques must be carefully solicited, however, so that participants' confidence is enhanced and not weakened.

6. A workshop on training skills should include the following concepts:

   Adult-learning theory. Adult learners, especially those who have not taken classes for several years, need support from their trainers.

   Leadership skills. Success in training ultimately depends on the trainer's ability to encourage learner participation and to guide meaningful group discussions.

   Training design. Trainers should be able to select methods that are suited to particular training needs.

   Administration and logistics. Trainers should know how to select participants, determine the most appropriate schedule, and make effective use of visual aids.

   Practice sessions. Participants should be able to practice new skills before an audience.

   Evaluation and follow-up. The ability to determine the effectiveness of training programs is a critical but often overlooked skill.

7. Trainers-in-training learn by example and by doing. By attending workshops and seminars, they have an opportunity to observe other

trainers and to improve their technique. Their first presentations should be carefully reviewed and evaluated by more experienced trainers.

8. Trainers need recognition from their managers as well as from participants in the program. Their efforts can be recognized in organization newsletters and should be considered during performance evaluations and merit-pay determinations.

19 Definitions of Staff Development: A Sampling

Frances O. Painter

Libraries are experiencing unprecedented changes in technology, clientele, services, and organization. Learning must be a continuing process for all library personnel, from the director to entry-level staff. Organizations want productivity, improved service, and effective use of resources. Individuals seek opportunities to learn, to keep up, to be recognized. A staff-development program brings these needs together and seeks to improve the effectiveness of library personnel.

A library's definition of staff development serves several purposes. A definition (or lack of one) communicates the philosophy of the library administration toward continuing staff-development programs and determines the role of planners, supervisors, and participants. A definition also provides a framework for evaluation of staff-development efforts. Without thoughtful attention to goals and desired outcomes, the success of staff development tends to be measured in terms of the number of attendees or number of workshops presented rather than in terms of needs met, problems solved, or efficiencies gained.

On the following pages are examples of definitions of staff development. Although they vary in length and coverage and represent different kinds of libraries, they lay the foundation for successful staff-development programs. For other examples, write to:

Staff Development Clearinghouse
ALA Headquarters Information Center
50 East Huron Street
Chicago, IL 60611

UNIVERSITY OF CALIFORNIA AT BERKELEY LIBRARY

Staff Development Program Statement

Program Definition and Goals

The General Library's mission is to support the instructional, research, and service programs of the University of California at Berkeley through the development of the Library's collections and the provision of information services. Because the success of this enterprise rests, ultimately, on the performance of the staff, it is important that each staff member have the skills, knowledge, and commitment necessary to provide appropriate levels of service. Staff development is an integral part of the Library's efforts to fulfill its mission.

The Library's Staff Development Program provides opportunities for individuals to expand their knowledge and experience in the library and information field. Participation in the Staff Development Program, unlike many other training and development programs, is staff-initiated. Employees are encouraged to take advantage of those opportunities that further their development, while meeting the needs of the Library.

Flexibility, perspective, and broad knowledge are valued assets in library work, a field that is affected by technology and economic realities. The Staff Development Program enables staff members to develop a range of skills within, and a broader perspective of their area of work—thus creating a more versatile staff better able to meet the changing needs of the University Community.

Scope

The Library's Staff Development Program includes opportunities for development through participation in the following activities:
1. In-house training sessions and workshops covering a broad range of skills and topics designed to improve job performance
2. Paid attendance at courses offered by Campus Personnel
3. Rotational opportunities
4. Committee and task-force work offering opportunities for broadening experience, as well as contributing to library programs
5. Teaching in the School of Library and Information Studies
6. Support for individual and group research projects provided by campus funds
7. Reduced-fee attendance at regular University courses
8. Individual financial support for approved attendance at off-campus workshops of career-related interest
9. Programs developed and offered by the Staff Development Committee

Responsibility

Responsibility for the implementation, continuity, and success of the program is shared:
1. The Library Administration, with the advice and support of the Staff Development Committee, is responsible for the planning, coordination, and evaluation of the program.
    a. The Library Personnel Office orients new employees toward benefits and general working conditions, coordinates training and development opportunities outside the Library, and offers career-development counseling.
    b. The Library Education Office assists in developing programs that upgrade skills needed by staff in the performance of their jobs.
    c. The Staff Development Committee advises the University Librarian on matters of staff development, organizes programs of interest to the library staff at large, and reviews funding and leaves requests made by General Library staff for career-related conferences and workshops. The committee acts as a clearinghouse for suggestions made by all staff for programs related to staff development.
    d. The LAUC-B Committee on Research and Professional Activities and Development reviews and recommends research allocations and professional activity funding requests for librarians on the Berkeley campus.

2. Library Department and Unit Heads are responsible for training staff to meet their job responsibilities; this must also include:
   a. Encouraging staff participation in staff development and continuing education activities that support the staff member's and department's goals
   b. Advising individual staff members on career goals and directions
   c. Interpreting staff and career development policies
   d. Promoting employee training and development opportunities
3. Supervisors act as information links between staff and Department Heads regarding the staff-development needs and goals of their units. They foster staff development within the constraints imposed by the need to accomplish unit goals.
4. All library staff members have the responsibility for monitoring their own growth and development, alerting their supervisors to specific training and development opportunities and participating in such activities.

Participation

All library staff members—career, casual, temporary—will receive training appropriate to their particular job assignments. Staff in career positions who have completed the probationary period and academic staff with career or potential career status are eligible for—and encouraged to participate in—staff-development activities.

PALATINE PUBLIC LIBRARY DISTRICT, PALATINE, ILLINOIS

Statement Defining Staff Development

The purpose of staff development at the Palatine Public Library District is to provide the opportunity for staff to learn, improve and update skills, create staff awareness of current issues which affect the library, and foster personal growth and a well-managed library by broadening perspectives.

REGENT UNIVERSITY LIBRARY, VIRGINIA BEACH, VIRGINIA

Staff Development Program—
Library Philosophy/Responsibility

Regent University Library administration encourages professional and support staff to develop their skills, capabilities, knowledge, and attitudes in order to mutually benefit the organizational effectiveness and the quality of library service by improved staff performance as well as greater satisfaction and opportunity for the individual.

Staff development includes a broad range of activities that are directly related to the staff members' role and responsibility in the library organization. It is a continuing process that orients, trains, and develops each member of the library organization. Some aspects of continuing education may be included; however, continuing education usually focuses on the needs of the individual rather than on the needs of the organization.

The responsibility for staff development rests mainly with library administration and supervisors but must also be shared by individual employees in order to be effective.

The library administration will plan and provide opportunities to meet development needs, inform the staff of these opportunities, and encourage the appropriate staff to take advantage of the activities and programs. Library policies and guidelines will aid in creating and maintaining a positive environment for growth and development. All staff members share a responsibility to take advantage of these opportunities, encourage others, and inform the library administration or supervisors of development needs.

A planned program of staff development will include orientation, in-service training, performance appraisal, and other activities. The library should benefit in the following ways: support of library goals, efficient use of resources, better service, improved staff morale, and more creative and capable employees. The staff should be able to broaden their vision, improve their ability, prepare for change, and take advantage of new career opportunities.

The Staff Development Committee and Associate Dean will assist in identifying staff needs, coordinate and assist with program presentations, help prepare training and program materials, advise regarding policies and procedures, and aid in evaluation of the staff development programs.

THE UNIVERSITY OF TEXAS AT AUSTIN GENERAL LIBRARIES

Staff Development Policy

Staff development is a continual process used to guide and encourage staff members to develop their skills, capabilities, knowledge and attitudes in order to mutually benefit both the organization and the individual. The ultimate goal is improvement in organizational effectiveness and the quality of library service by improved staff performance.

The library administration strongly supports staff development and considers it an integral part of the overall library program. Time committed to staff-development activities is well spent, insuring that staff members have the opportunity to develop and hence be more able to contribute to existing operations and to accommodate technological and organizational change. With two-thirds of the General Libraries dedicated to staff costs, staff development is an investment which benefits both the General Libraries and The University of Texas at Austin.

The responsibility for staff development rests most heavily on library administration and supervisors, but is also shared by individual employees. Responsibilities at the administrative and supervisory levels ensure (1) that opportunities are provided to meet developmental needs, (2) that staff are informed of opportunities, (3) that appropriate staff are strongly encouraged to take advantage of opportunities, and (4) that, through General Libraries policies and guidelines and a positive managerial attitude, an atmosphere is created and maintained in which the development of individual potential can thrive. All staff members share a responsibility for availing themselves of opportunities, for encouraging each other, and for making their development needs known.

RIVERSIDE CITY AND COUNTY PUBLIC LIBRARY, CALIFORNIA

Staff Development, Continuing Education, and Training Policy and Procedure

Definition of Staff Development. The Library is responsible for the development of its staff members' capabilities through the provision of orientation, in-service training, opportunities for participation in professional associations, encouragement of community involvement, and, within policy and budget constraints, provision of paid time, schedule adjustments, and reimbursement for job-related workshops and other training opportunities. When changes are made in job assignments, the Library is responsible for providing the necessary in-service training.

The Library is also responsible for encouraging employees to take responsibility for their own continuing education and for providing a climate in which this is possible.

Staff development for which the Library is responsible and continuing education for which the individual staff member is responsible are mutually complimentary. Acceptance of our responsibilities for them will result in better library service to the people of Riverside City and County.

Policy. It is the policy of the Library to make employees aware of training opportunities which will improve their ability to perform their present jobs and prepare themselves for promotional opportunities. Supervisors should be aware of their responsibility to assist in the development of those working under their supervision. This is in the best interests of both the Library and the individuals involved.

INDIANA UNIVERSITY LIBRARIES—BLOOMINGTON

Faculty-Staff Development Policy

Program Definition

The mission of the Indiana University Libraries is to provide access to information and materials to support the teaching, research and service of faculty and students. Because the success of this enterprise rests ultimately on the effectiveness of faculty and staff, it is important that each member have the skills, knowledge, and commitment necessary to provide appropriate levels of service. Faculty and staff development is an integral part of the Library's efforts to fulfill its mission.

Flexibility, perspective, and broad knowledge are valued assets in library work, a field that is affected by technology and economic realities. The faculty and staff development program enable individuals to develop a range of skills within, and a broader perspective of their area of work—thus creating a more versatile faculty and staff better able to meet the changing needs of the University and Library communities.

Goals

A. To provide opportunities to expand library skills and knowledge in order to enhance job performance.

B. To provide opportunities that enable library faculty and staff to improve skills not necessarily related to their present positions in an effort to aid in preparing for advancement.

C. To provide greater organizational effectiveness through increased awareness among faculty and staff of the interrelationships and functions of the various activities and services of the Libraries.

D. To provide training that promotes faculty and staff to versatility in a work environment that is responsive to changing technology.

E. To provide training that fosters personal and long range development.

MASSACHUSETTS INSTITUTE OF TECHNOLOGY LIBRARIES

Staff Development

Definition

Staff Development in the MIT Libraries is a program in which a variety of activities is undertaken to improve the effectiveness of individuals and/or groups in carrying out their present responsibilities or to prepare them for potential future responsibilities in the MIT Libraries. These activities may, in addition, contribute toward the achievement of career goals.

UNIVERSITY OF MICHIGAN LIBRARIES

Staff Development Policy

The Library Staff Development Program provides staff members with support for acquiring the knowledge and skills necessary to perform effectively in current and future assignments in the Library.

Staff development includes three components:

Orientation. New employees are introduced to the unit and Library organization and working environment, and to the University.

Training. Employees are familiarized with knowledge and skills necessary to perform specific responsibilities effectively.

Development. Employees are introduced to broad concepts and general background and techniques necessary to assume new and higher level responsibilities and to respond positively to change.

Activities in the program are both formal and informal. Typical activities include orientation sessions, training workshops presented in the Library, programs offered by the University Human Resources Development Office, and coursework supported through the Tuition Refund Program.

20 How to Learn More and Keep Up: A Guide to Bibliographic Resources

J. Linda Williams, with June Breland, Deborah A. Carver, Dominique Coulombe, Patricia Finney, and Charles E. Kratz

The intention of this guide is to provide you with practical information on staff development. Once a staff-development program is in effect, you will want to consult additional resources to gain further information and to keep abreast of current trends and activities in the field. This section has been included to assist you in locating additional information on staff development.

Where to Look

The following call numbers and terms will yield productive information.

Library of Congress call numbers:
HF5549
HF5549.5
Z668
Z668.5
Dewey call numbers:
020.7/15
023.8
658.3/12404
658.3/01
Library of Congress subject headings:
Assessment centers (personnel-management procedures)
Educational technology
Employees—In-service training
Employees—Training of

Employer supported education
Instructional systems—Design
Librarians—In-service training/education
Library education
Library education (Continuing education)
Library personnel management
Management—Study and teaching
Occupational training
Personnel management
Library Literature subject headings
College and university librarians—education
Continuing education
In-service education
Institutes and workshops
Paraprofessionals—training
Public librarians—education

Current Journals

Many periodicals published outside the library field contain valuable information on the subject of staff development. The most pertinent ones are listed here.

Academy of Management. 1958– . Quarterly. Scholarly publication reporting on empirical research into psychological and sociological factors affecting the workplace. Most articles deal with organizational behavior.

Academy of Management Review. 1976– . Quarterly. Specializes in interpretive articles on organizational and management theory.

Administration in Social Work. 1977– . Quarterly. Staff development and management issues in human service organizations.

Administrative Science Quarterly. 1956– . Quarterly. Lengthy, scholarly articles emphasizing issues in public administration.

Harvard Business Review. 1922– . Bimonthly. General readership; special emphasis on management issues and innovation in the workplace.

HRMagazine. 1990– . Monthly. A wide variety of topics from different sectors, including education; practical advise on hiring, supervising, and evaluating.

Human Resource Planning. 1978– . Quarterly. Practical applications of human resource planning research; themes include career management, performance appraisal, and personnel ethics.

Journal of Applied Behavioral Science. 1965– . Quarterly. In-depth articles on organizational development, group dynamics, and evaluative techniques; heavy emphasis on planning for organizational change.

Journal of Employment Counseling. 1964– . Quarterly. Topics include job retraining, problems of special worker groups, career planning, and job satisfaction; describes programs and workshops on interviewing skills, and communication skills.

Journal of Management Development. 1982– . Bimonthly. Specialized articles emphasize management training and development, and getting the right people into the right job.

Management Review. 1923– . Monthly. Short articles on timely issues aimed at upper management; problem-solving tone.

Personnel. 1919– Monthly. Practical as well as theoretical aspects of personnel management, with an emphasis on the private sector; topics include job satisfaction, employee training, and job redesign.

Personnel Journal. 1922– . Monthly. Aimed at the practitioner. Style is less scholarly than many academic journals; spotlights important trends such as teamwork, motivation, and smoking and health in the workplace.

Personnel Management. 1920– . Monthly. A slightly British bias, focusing on issues concerning unemployment, retraining, and collective bargaining.

Personnel Psychology. 1948– . Quarterly. Articles are useful for anyone involved in personnel management; topics cover work attitudes, productivity, and behavioral problems.

Public Personnel Management. 1940– . Quarterly. A practical approach to problems in public administration; articles written by academics covering issues such as merit pay, drug testing, and training methods.

SAM Advanced Management Journal. 1935– . Quarterly. Business-school journal covering general topics of interest to middle managers, educators, and students; a "how-to" tone on topics such as "motivating the older worker."

Sloan Management Review. 1960– . Quarterly. Management issues presented from a slightly theoretical perspective; scholarly but readable.

Supervisory Management. 1989– . Monthly. Short, pragmatic articles concerning leadership delegation, employee discipline, and report writing; aimed at the first-level supervisor.

Training. 1964– . Monthly. Short, practical articles on methods and techniques of training personnel; includes many examples of training programs.

Training and Development Journal. 1945– . Monthly. Special emphasis on communication matters, management training programs, time management, and dealing with change.

Clearinghouse

The LAMA PAS Staff Development Committee maintains a clearinghouse of staff development programs. For examples of programs that have been implemented in libraries, write to:

Staff Development Clearinghouse
ALA Headquarters Information Center
50 East Huron Street
Chicago, IL 60611

Staff-Development Bibliography and Reading List

How to Get Started

Abella, Kay Tytler. *Building Successful Training Programs: A Step-by Step Guide.* Reading, Mass.: Addison-Wesley, 1985.

Association of Research Libraries. Office of Management Studies. Systems and Procedures Exchange Center. *Staff Development* SPEC Kits and Flyers, number 75 (1981).

Buchanan, W. Wray, Frank Hoy, and Bobby C. Vaught. "Any Development Program Can Work." *Personnel Journal* 64 (June 1985): 62–67.

Condon, Mary, ed. "How Do You Start a Training/HRD Department from Scratch?" *Training and Development Journal* 39 (August 1985): 12–20.

Conroy, Barbara. *Learning Packaged to Go: Directory and Guide to Staff Development and Training Packages.* Phoenix, Ariz.: Oryx Press, 1983.

Conroy, Barbara. *Library Staff Development and Continuing Education: Principles and Practices.* Littleton, Colo.: Libraries Unlimited, 1983.

Craig, Robert L., ed. *Training and Development Handbook: A Guide to Human Resource Development.* 3d ed. New York: McGraw-Hill, 1987.

Creth, Shelia D. *Effective On-the-Job Training.* Chicago: American Library Association, 1986.

Martin, Murray S. *Issues in Personnel Management in Academic Libraries.* Greenwich, Conn.: JAI Press, 1981.

Prytherch, Ray. *Handbook of Library Training Practice.* Hants, England: Gower, 1986.

Rosenberg, Jane A. *Resource Notebook on Staff Development.* Washington, D.C.: Office of Management Studies, Association of Research Libraries, 1983.

Tenopir, Carol. "In-House Training and Staff Development." *Library Journal* 109 (May 1984): 870–71.

How to Gather Support

Bennett, Barbara, and David F. Griswold. "Providing Our Worth: The Training Value Model." *Training and Development Journal* 38 (October 1984): 81–83.

Krayer, Karl J. "Using Training to Reduce Role Conflict and Ambiguity." *Training and Development Journal* 40 (November 1986): 49-52.

Lawrie, John. "Prove to Management that Training Works." *Personnel Journal* 63 (December 1984): 64–65.

Magnus, Margaret. "Training Futures." *Personnel Journal* 65 (May 1986): 60–71.

Wehrenberg, Stephen B. "Supervisors as Trainers: The Long-term Gains of OJT." *Personnel Journal* 66 (April 1987): 48–51.

How to Identify Staff Needs

Apking, Ann M., and Laura Fleming. "The Need for a Needs Analysis." *Telephone Engineer and Management* (March 1986): 72–73.

Birnbrauer, Herman, and Lynne A. Tyson. "How to Analyze Needs." *Training and Development Journal* 39 (August 1985): 53–58.

Brinkerhoff, Robert O. "Expanding Needs Analysis." *Training and Development Journal* 40 (February 1986): 64–65.

Brown, F. Gerald, and Kenneth R. Wedel. *Assessing Training Needs.* Washington, D.C.: National Training and Development Service Press, 1984.

Cureton, James, Alfred F. Neton, and Dennis G. Teslowski. "Finding Out What Managers Need." *Training and Development Journal* 40 (May 1986): 106–7.

Fleming, Laura, and Ann M. Apking. "Training: Do You Need Analysis?" *Audio-Visual Communications* (February 1986): 44–45, 49.

Georgenson, Dave, and Edward Del Gaizo. "Maximize the Return on Your Training Investment through Needs Analysis." *Training and Development Journal* 38 (August 1984): 42–47.

Jones, Noragh, and Peter Jordon. "Staff Training and Development." In *Staff Management in Library and Information Work,* 172–94. Hampshire, England: Gower, 1982.

Kaman, Vicki S. "Why Assessment Interviews Are Worth It." *Training and Development Journal* 40 (May 1986): 108–10.

Lampe, Steven. "Getting the Most Out of Needs Assessments." *Training* (October 1986): 101–4.

Pecora, Peter J., Steven Paul Schinke, and James K. Whittaker. "Needs Assessment for Staff Training." *Administration in Social Work* 7 (Fall–Winter 1983): 101–13.

Smith, Barry, Brian Delahaye, and Peter Gates. "Some Observations on TNA." *Training and Development Journal* 40 (August 1986): 63–68.

"The Supervisor's Role in a Training Needs Analysis." *Supervisory Management* 31 (May 1986): 40–42.

How to Set Goals

Cafferella, Rosemary S. "A Checklist for Planning Successful Training Programs." *Training and Development Journal* 39 (March 1985): 81–83.

Kirkpatrick, Donald L. "Effective Supervisory Training and Development. Part I: Responsibility, Needs and Objectives." *Personnel* 61 (November–December 1984): 25-30.

Lawrie, John. "Skill Inventories: Pack for the Future." *Personnel Journal* 66 (March 1987): 127–30.

Stueart, Robert D. "Preparing Libraries for Change." *Library Journal* 109 (September 1984): 1724–26.

How to Pay for Programs

Kozoll, Charles E. *Staff Development in Organizations: A Cost Evaluation Manual for Managers and Trainers.* Reading, Mass.: Addison-Wesley, 1974.

"Professional Development: Who Pays for What?" *Training* 22 (August 1985): 10.

Spenser, Lyle G. "How to Calculate the Cost and Benefits of an HRD Program." *Training* 20 (July 1984): 40–44 passim.

Varlejs, Jana. "Cost Models for Staff Development in Academic Libraries." *Journal of Academic Librarianship* 12 (January 1987): 359–64.

Zemke, Ron, Linda Standke, and Philip Jones. *Designing and Delivering Cost-Effective Training—and Measuring the Results.* Minneapolis, Minn.: Lakewood Publications, 1981.

How to Find Expert Speakers or Presenters

"How to Contract for Speaker Insurance before the Meeting." *Training* 23 (July 1986): 13–14.

"How to Shop for the Right Seminar." *Training* 23 (June 1986): 17ff.

How to Prepare for Specific Programs, Improve Your Visual Aids, and Make an Effective Presentation

Buckley, Marilyn Hanf, and Owen Boyle. *Mapping the Writing Journey.* Berkeley, Calif.: Bay Area Writing Project, University of California, 1981.

Carnegie, Dorothy. *Effective Speaking.* (A revision of *Public Speaking and Influencing Men in Business* by Dale Carnegie.) New York.

Communication Briefings. Glassboro, New Jersey. (A monthly journal of "ideas that work," including practical tips on speaking, persuasion, public relations, and other relevant topics.)

Eitington, Julius E. *The Winning Trainer.* Houston: Gulf Publishing Co., 1984.

Graphically Speaking: How to Prepare a Visual Presentation. Chicago: Arthur Andersen & Co., 1983.

Speaking Out: How to Prepare and Give a Speech. Chicago: Arthur Andersen & Co., 1983.

Watzman, Suzanne. "Presentation with Power." *ITC Desktop* (March–April 1989): 32ff.

How to Make Training Stick

Ehrenberg, Lyle M. "How to Ensure Better Transfer of Learning." *Training and Development Journal* 37 (February 1983): 81–83.

Kelley, Ann I., Robert F. Orgel, and Donald M. Baer. "Seven Strategies That Guarantee Training Transfer." *Training and Development Journal* 39 (November 1985): 78–82.

Leifer, Mellissa S., and John W. Newstrom. "Solving the Transfer of Training Problem." *Training and Development Journal* 34 (August 1980): 42–46.

Marx, Robert D. "Relapse Prevention for Managerial Training: A Model for Maintenance of Behavior Change." *Academy of Management* 7 (June 1982): 433–41.

Marx, Robert D. "Self-Managed Skill Retention." *Training and Development Journal* 40 (January 1986): 54–57.

Mosel, James N. "Why Training Programs Fail to Carry Over." *Personnel* 34 (November–December 1957): 56–64.

Newstrom, John W. "Leveraging Management Development Through the Management of Transfer." *Journal of Management Development* 5, no. 5 (1986): 33–45.

Noe, Raymond A., Jalanta Sears, and Angela M. Fullenkamp. "Relapse Training: Does it Influence Trainees' Post Training Behavior and Cognitive Strategies?" *Journal of Business and Psychology* 4 (Spring 1990): 317–28.

Schendel, Joel D., and Joseph D. Hagman. "On Sustaining Procedural Skills over a Prolonged Retention Interval." *Journal of Applied Psychology* 67 (October 1982): 605–10.

Trost, Arty. "They May Love It but Will They Use It?" *Training and Development Journal* 39 (January 1985): 78–81.

Wexley, Kenneth, and Timothy Baldwin. "Posttraining Strategies for Facilitating Positive Transfer: An Empirical Exploration." *Academy of Management Journal* 29 (September 1986): 503–20.

How to Evaluate Your Program

Quinn, Susan R., and Shelley Karp. "Developing an Objective Evaluation Tool." *Training and Development Journal* 40 (May 1986): 90–92.

Swierezek, Frederick William, and Lynne Carmichael. "The Quantity and Quality of Evaluative Training." *Training and Development* 39 (January 1985): 95–99.

How to Develop Training Skills

Brookfield, Stephen, ed. *Training Educators of Adults*. London: Routledge, 1988.

Brookfield, Stephen. *Understanding and Facilitating Adult Learning*. San Francisco: Jossey-Bass, 1986.

Daloz, Laurent A. *Effective Teaching and Mentoring*. San Francisco: Jossey-Bass, 1986.

Ellis, Steven K. *How to Survive a Training Assignment*. Reading, Mass.: Addison-Wesley, 1988.

Munson, Lawrence S. *How to Conduct Training Seminars*. New York: McGraw-Hill, 1984.

Nilson, Carolyn D. *Training for Non-trainers*. New York: AMACOM, 1991.

Contributors

Lynn C. Badger, formerly library personnel officer, is now Biological Sciences selector at University of Florida Libraries in Gainesville.

June Breland is branch librarian of the College of Veterinary Medicine at Mississippi State University.

Deborah A. Carver is assistant university librarian for public services at the University of Oregon in Eugene, Oregon. She has written several staff development essays for *Library Administration and Management Journal* and has served as past chair of the LAMA PAS Staff Development Committee.

John Cochenour has recently accepted a position at the University of Wyoming, School of Education, as an instructional technologist. He is also an adjunct professor at the University of Oklahoma's School of Library Science.

Dominique Coulombe is head of the Catalog Department at Brown University Library in Providence, Rhode Island.

Patricia Finney is head of stack maintenance at the Center for Research Libraries in Chicago.

Kenna Forsyth is staff development specialist at the Baltimore County Library. She is active in LAMA's Personnel Administration Section and the CLENE Round Table and serves on several Maryland statewide training and continuing education committees.

Susan Jurow is director of the Office of Management Services, Association of Research Libraries, in Washington, D.C., which provides training and consulting in public services and library management for academic and research libraries. Among the many programs she has helped to design and present are the Training Skills Institute, the Creativity to Innovation Workshop, and the Project Planning Workshop.

Eva L. Kiewitt, associate dean of libraries at Regent University Library in

Virginia Beach, Virginia, has written books and articles in the areas of information science and education.

Charles E. Kratz is assistant dean of public services at Hofstra University Library in Hempstead, New York. He is co-editor of the LAMA publication *Training Issues in Changing Technology.*

Anne Grodzins Lipow is a library consultant, specializing in organizational management, staff training and user services; until 1991 she was director of library education at the University of California, Berkeley, Library. She is a frequent lecturer and writer on aspects of staff development, electronic information resources, and organizational change.

Frances O. Painter is assistant director for personnel and public services at the University Libraries of Virginia Polytechnic Institute and State University in Blacksburg, Virginia. She is co-editor of *Training Issues and Strategies in Libraries* (Haworth Press, 1990).

Janet T. Paulk is library personnel officer at Emory University Library in Atlanta. She wrote "General Libraries Personnel Survey Team Report and Long Range Plan" (Emory University, 1980/81), published in the 1981 ARL SPEC Kit on Staff Development.

Wendy L. Scott is library personnel officer at the University of Florida Libraries, Gainesville.

Kitty Smith is assistant professor, University of North Carolina–Greensboro, Department of Library and Information Studies. Her most recent articles are (by Catherine Smith) "Checking Employment References— Can I Get What I Really Need?" *Library Personnel News* (Fall 1987) and (with co-author Jeanne M. Isacco) "Hiring: A Common Sense Approach," *Journal of Library Administration* (Summer 1985).

Pat L. Weaver-Meyers is head of Access Services Department, University of Oklahoma. Her recent publications include "ARL Libraries and Staff Development: A Suggested Model for Success" in *College & Research Libraries* and *Interlibrary Loan in Academic and Research Libraries: Workload and Staffing* (Occasional Paper no. 15) Office of Management Services, ARL. She is also consultant and ACRL-CE course presenter for "Accommodating Change through Training and Staff Development."

J. Linda Williams is staff specialist in school library media services and educational technology at the Maryland State Department of Education in Baltimore. She is past chair of the LAMA PAS Staff Development Committee.

Index

Compiled by Pamela Hori